The Coming
DARK AGE

THE COMING

Dark Age

ROBERTO VACCA

TRANSLATED FROM THE ITALIAN BY
DR. J. S. WHALE

DOUBLEDAY & COMPANY, INC.

GARDEN CITY, NEW YORK

1973

IL MEDIOEVO PROSSIMO VENTURO by Roberto Vacca © Arnoldo
Mondadori Editore 1971

JUN 17 '75

ISBN: 0-385-06340-7
Library of Congress Catalog Card Number 73–81118
Translation Copyright © 1973 by Doubleday & Company, Inc.
All Rights Reserved
Printed in the United States of America
First Edition

Contents

	Introduction	1
I	Reaching the Knee of the Curve	7
II	Is a Halt to Expansion Unlikely?	19
III	Large Systems and Their Engineering	33
IV	Large Systems Getting Out of Control	47
V	The Powerless Electricians	61
VI	Urban Congestion and Traffic Paralysis	73
VII	Crisis in Communications	93
VIII	Electronic Computers: Some Unjustified Hopes and Fears	107
IX	Water and Waste	125
X	Death of the City of New York	131
XI	Is Modern War Irrelevant to the Issue?	141
XII	The Futility of Protest	149
XIII	The Crisis of Management	159
XIV	The Beginning and Duration of the Dark Age	169
XV	Short-Term Gains and Long-Term Losses	177
XVI	Social Life Before and After the Knockout	185
XVII	Foundations of a New Tradition	197
XVIII	Monastic Communities Looking Backward and Forward	207
	Notes	223

The Coming
DARK AGE

Introduction

And I saw an angel come down from heaven, having the key of the bottomless pit and a great chain in his hand.

And he laid hold on the dragon, that old serpent, which is the Devil, and Satan, and bound him a thousand years,

And cast him into the bottomless pit, and shut him up, and set a seal upon him, that he should deceive the nations no more, till the thousand years should be fulfilled: and after that he must be loosed a little season.

And I saw thrones, and they sat upon them, and judgment was given unto them: and I saw the souls of them that were beheaded for the witness of Jesus, and for the word of God, and which had not worshipped the beast, neither his image, neither had received his mark upon their foreheads, or in their hands; and they lived and reigned with Christ a thousand years.

But the rest of the dead lived not again until the thousand years were finished. This is the first resurrection.

The Apocalypse of St. John the Divine, 20:1–5

This passage from the Apocalypse once convinced multi-tudes of people that the world would come to an end in the year A.D. 1000. Feeling doomed and powerless, they sought refuge and pardon in prayer and penitence. The able-bodied lost innumerable working hours, spending on their knees time that they had formerly given to productive work. Then the year 1000 passed, and the world did not come to an end—a notable fact that nevertheless did not modify the apocalyptic beliefs and superstitions in any way. Indeed, in the centuries that followed there were many other occasions when astrologers and numerologists predicted cataclysm and ruin. While cataclysm and ruin have not been absent during recent centuries, they have turned out to be in actual fact rather different from the improvised anticipations of the prophets.

I am writing when the second millennium of our era is less than thirty years from completion and when, for reasons different from those of a thousand years ago, many people expect that before long there will be tragic and to-tal catastrophe. Today's prophets do not tell us to fear angels, dragons, or the abyss. We have to fear nuclear holocaust, overpopulation, pollution, and ecological dis-aster.

Writers who announce imminent catastrophe are today so numerous that John Crosby has invented a new term to describe their activity: doom-writing. In an article in *The Observer* of September 13, 1970, he contended that catastrophes thus announced never come true and that conditions of life in cities and in the world have never been better than they are now. Railing at the doom-writers, he accuses them of a pessimism both fashionable and lucrative: they urge opinions that are readily acceptable and sell profitably.

But there must be many who agree with the doom-writers, since it is commonly assumed that the population of the world will be 6 billion in the year 2000. Indeed, specialists in this field affirm that thirty years hence the world's population will be more than double what it is now (it is now estimated to be 3½ billion). Fred Charles Iklé, of the Massachusetts Institute of Technology, has stated that in 2000 "the world's population will be some 7 or 8 billion rather than 5"—a modification of the figure estimated in 1963 by the Rand Corporation.

Though agreement about these population forecasts is virtually unanimous, I am convinced that time will not confirm them. There are several factors indicating that the present rate at which human numbers are growing and human structures developing may soon slow to a stop and go into reverse.

It is not necessary for a few kilomegatons of hydrogen bombs to explode for hundreds of millions of people to be killed. The same result may occur by less violent and more intricate means: that is, by virtue of the fact that vast concentrations of human beings are involved in systems that are now so complicated that they are becoming uncontrollable. This hypothesis—of an apocalypse that is impersonal, casual, and unpremeditated—is more tragic than the other.

This book is an attempt to analyze one type of catastrophe that could come about through the breakdown of the great systems that are now becoming so extremely complicated. My thesis is that our great technological systems of human organization and association are continuously outgrowing ordered control: they are now reaching critical dimensions of instability. As yet, a crisis in a single system would not be enough to bring a great metropolitan concentration to a halt. But a chance concomitance of stoppages in the same area could start a catastrophic process that would paralyze the most developed societies and lead to the deaths of millions of people.

A few chapters describe breakdowns that are already under way in systems for the production and distribution of power: for transportation, communication, water supply, the disposal of waste, and the processing of information. Such crises are due to the chronic congestion of almost all large systems—so often poorly designed and set up or (worse still) allowed to proliferate at random because ability at the top has been inadequate, and requisite information as to present needs and future trends unavailable.

One cannot demonstrate *a priori*, of course, that a chance coincidence of events—decline, congestion, and slow-down—must lead inevitably to disaster: not, at least, in a developing situation such as I describe. It seems very likely, however, that the most developed nations are on the way toward breakdown on a large scale. It seems to me sound procedure to accept certain assumptions and to deduce their logical consequences in detail, in order to show realistically what the imminent dangers are. I have used the term "dark age"—"Dark Ages" was the term often applied to the early medieval era from, say, 500 to 1100—to describe this coming widespread crisis.

Countries that are less advanced than others (either on the way to modernity, or still underdeveloped, or just backward) will only be involved in the crisis to a marginal extent. Seventy per cent of the population of the world will not be much injured by the first wave of destruction. On the other hand, the more advanced nations will be more vulnerable to the harm that will accompany the breakdown of the great systems: in the dark age that would follow, their total population might be halved. Since these nations would include Europe and the Soviet Union, North America and Japan, some 900 million people would be involved, or about 30 per cent of the present population of the world.

The death of 450 million people in the world's most developed countries would mean that scientific development, technological research, large undertakings in civil engineering, industrial mass production at low cost, the whole organizing and directive structures that function in modern society, would come to a complete stop. Along with a certain setback that the countries of the third world would suffer, there would be grave secondary consequences: manufactured goods, finished and durable products, medicines, production facilities and managerial know-how previously supplied by the more advanced nations—all would be missing.

Because of these presuppositions, recovery will be slow and difficult; and on the road toward reconstruction, countries will not necessarily be in the lead because they were so once upon a time. New primacies and hierarchies among the peoples of the world will be decided by the availability of know-how and by the ability to find new and effective forms of social and organized life. And, by the capacity that various groups of people may show for decision and aggression. But the coming dark age will not last as long as the Dark Ages of early medieval times, now long past: it will last perhaps a century.

We cannot know whether future historians will fix on 1960, 1970, or some later date for its beginning: it would seem from many signs that the era of breakdown may have started already. Thus there is nothing absurd in the three-fold assumption that, first, an era of disorder and destruction is coming; second, that it is imminent; third, that it will be followed by rebirth. The third assumption has no justification other than the periodic alternation of all things human, which history seems to support.

Accustomed in this twentieth century to considering change as the most constant feature of our world, we like to anticipate what changes will take place next. In his book *The Unveiling of the Future*[1] Richard Lewinsohn shows that today we are much better at forecasting and planning ahead than we used to be. My belief that he has proved his point justifies my writing about a middle age which is still at its beginning. To accuse me of doom-writing and pessimism will be easy enough. But we pessimists call our way of looking at things "realism," and we do not regard ourselves as any less effective than the optimists in preparing remedies and in planning reforms.

Rome, February 1970–March 1973

Reaching the Knee of the Curve

Imagine driving a big truck on an uphill road. The slope is becoming steeper and your speed is decreasing. You shift down to the lowest gear, the engine is laboring, the slope is getting worse. But with so heavy a vehicle and so powerful an engine there seems to be no danger of losing traction. Still, the hood is all the time getting higher in your field of vision and seems almost vertical. The slope steepens more. To turn back now is out of the question. Surely sooner or later the road will have to level off. In a cold sweat you ask yourself whether the truck will overturn.

A simile. It pictures those mathematical curves that represent the time variation in any number that measures some aspect of our civilization. Everything grows: everything is on the increase, and every year the speed of that increase is greater. For example:

The population of the world was 800 million in 1750, 1,200 million in 1850, 2,400 million in 1950, and in 1973 it is well over 3,600 million.

The maximum speed of vehicles was 35 miles per hour in 1850, 100 m.p.h. in 1900, 1000 m.p.h. in 1950, and now astronauts travel at a speed of some 24,840 m.p.h.

Similar growth rates are shown by the expanding highway systems, the number of telephones, the number of travelers by air, the number of books printed annually—in short, the numerical membership of any and every class of object and activity.

All these measurements, then, have the character of continuous and exponential growth, and their variation obeys a well-known mathematical law, the law of the phenomenon of growth in the presence of limiting factors. At first the effect of these limiting factors is hardly noticeable, but there comes a time when they begin to predominate and to produce the phenomenon known as "saturation": the curve begins to look like a shoulder or knee. The result is a steady lessening of the curve's growing steepness until the steepness diminishes to the point where growth virtually ceases, measurement is constant, and the curve representing it continues as a straight horizontal line. The ascent is over. We have reached the crest.

The simile of a truck climbing a road of increasing steepness and running the risk of overturning before getting to the crest is not overdramatic. In fact, it is not the natural order for things always to run smoothly. Often the effect of the limiting factors is not felt gradually: it may be felt all of a sudden; instead of a rounded shoulder, there may be turbulent oscillations accompanied by disorder and breakdown. Indeed, the hypothesis that changes are uncomfortable, coming swiftly and violently, is more likely to prove true than the alternative hypothesis that they are tolerable because they come as gradual and slow transitions. Trying to foresee what the first hypothesis in all its grimness may involve is therefore well worthwhile. As Lewinsohn observed, we are all prophets, not so much from choice as from sheer necessity.

It is a curious fact that an investigation of this kind is not very popular. For, living as we do in advanced societies, we are so familiar with the ever growing numbers and the ever denser congestion of people, vehicles, machines, buildings, etc., that we have difficulty even in imagining situations that are different—static rather than progressive, contracting rather than expanding. We inevitably regard a slowdown, recession, or crisis as abnormal and transient. And it should be added in passing that this attitude is not unjustified: the past 150 years confirm it. They even allow us to conclude that planners are, if anything, too conservative, timidly underestimating future growth. Traditionally engineers and planners have tended to be out of date in the very fields in which they operate, ignoring the time lag between a project and its actual execution, and designing roads, telephone networks, and housing as though catering to the needs of ten years ago rather than to present and future needs.

There are a few notable exceptions. The name of Pierre Charles L'Enfant springs to mind at once—the army engineer who planned and designed with great foresight the city of Washington, D.C. The capital of the United States, conceived at the end of the eighteenth century, has functioned well for 150 years. That L'Enfant's work was harshly criticized in his day is not to be wondered at:

whenever anyone thinks on the grand scale, he is accused of being an extravagant showman.

It is not enough, however, simply to take note of the fact that the dimensions of a given problem are getting bigger. We have also to determine the laws by which this increase takes place, and by what different laws it will take place in the less immediate future.

Ill-equipped planners, unfortunately, work on childishly linear principles when forecasting the future—and then they realize, of course, that the real world has changed much faster than they expected. Even at a more competent level, where the laws of growth are known and expressed as simple mathematical formulas, it happens too often that better informed planners make use of unduly simplified statements of those laws, and make bad mistakes as a result.

This seems to suggest that any forecast is normally defective and inaccurate and to contradict the thesis with which we began—that sooner or later we will reach some kind of knee. Obviously we need to demonstrate and prove that present growth rates cannot possibly be maintained unchanged over a long period. Let us look, for example, at the indubitable problem for which remedies of various types are constantly being suggested: the population explosion.

Even if we use one of the more modest and prudent formulas that have been suggested as the law of growth for the population of the world, the conclusion to which it brings us is this: if continuously valid for the next two thousand years, it would give a world population of 150,000 billion people, i.e., one person to every square meter of the earth's surface (seas excluded). In the next eight thousand years it would give a population of 10^{23} (1 followed by 23 zeros) with a density of 666 million people to every square meter, or 62 million people to every square foot. Which is absurd. Incidentally, the weight of the whole terrestrial population would then be equal to that of the globe itself (including its heavy central nucleus, made up of nickel and iron). It is obvious that the limiting factors will be in action long before either (absurd) hypothetical target is reached.

But the action of limiting factors in our everyday experience of saturation is no hypothetical supposition. The growth of the total number of automobiles in different countries provides a typical example. In Italy the total number of cars doubles every four years. In the United States, on the other hand, the total number doubles every fifteen years—much more slowly. This means that in America the point representing this growth is to be found at a higher level and at a lower gradient on the exponential curve which tends to move toward its asymptotic constant: When the asymptote is reached, the number of cars will grow at approximately the same rate as the total population (assuming, of course, that the population will still be growing at that time). We can now look at two alternative possibilities.

First, assuming that the growth curves of population, facilities, and services (i.e., people's houses, their means of transport and communication) reach the knee gradually and smoothly, what disadvantages would this involve? It is highly probable that planning engineers would only then learn to plan and build in terms of the huge needs of the future and not in terms of the more modest needs of the past; but the disadvantage would be that imposing works would be undertaken to meet the estimated needs of a future growth which would, in fact, have passed its knee and be diminishing, if not already at a halt. Society would just be reaching equilibrium only to find that equilibrium disturbed by an excessive and wasteful use of resources on new constructions and services for which there was only a diminishing demand. It is possible, of course, that a situation such as this might develop simply through what Dickson Carr called "the cussedness of things in general." But there is nothing tragic in the possibility that planners and designers might strive to keep pace with the very rapid growth of society, gathering such momentum in doing so that—unable to apply the brakes in time—they would go far beyond the proper stopping place. Nor would it be the first time that wealth on a large scale had been wasted or frozen in the production of things that turned out to be superfluous or useless.

Second, it is much more interesting to consider the second more dangerous possibility—that the growth curves of the various parameters that measure our civilization will show marked *overshoots*: that is, they will show the parameter value first climbing much higher than the asymptotic equilibrium value, and then making a correspondingly steep descent; then a new climb followed by an equal and opposite descent; and so on until the oscillations die and equilibrium is reached. These overshoots occur when the limiting factors do not go into action in a continuous and balanced way as they should (like a governor on an engine), but are overborne or neutralized by booming expansion, until the moment comes when, by their cumulative action, they in their turn succeed in neutralizing the expansion. This type of problem can be tackled mathematically, though without any great improvement in the quality and range of one's forecasts. The use of formulas presupposes data not normally available in practice, as well as knowledge of the causal relationships of the phenomena under discussion such as we do not at present possess. Jay W. Forrester, of the Massachusetts Institute of Technology, has shown that in the field of complex systems, cause-to-effect relationships are very difficult to analyze: hardly ever does one given parameter depend on just one other factor. What happens is that all factors and parameters are interrelated by means of multiple feedback loops, the structure of which is far from obvious; so that only an accurate modeling of the system can bring us nearer to an understanding of the process.

It is of no great interest, however, to determine the number or the period of the oscillations mentioned above, mainly because their movements have no more than a theoretical model value; and because, in all probability, they will be hardly recognizable when other phenomena—at present unforeseeable—dominate the scene. There will be the cumulative action, too, of innumerable random events, which will cover any curve with "noise" even though it is plotted in accordance with theories sticking closely to reality.

The forecast that will serve as the basis for the considerations that follow is that at least one overshoot will occur. In other words, the size of the large systems will so far outgrow any position of stable and durable equilibrium that they will necessarily shrink and fall to levels much lower than those existing now. This book is concerned throughout with that dark breakdown: the imminent dark age. I define "dark age" as the period elapsing between the time in which maximum overshoot is reached and the time when the minimum is passed and a new period of expansion will begin.

It will be clear that I am not thinking here of a recession or of a crisis as admittedly grave as that of 1929, but of phenomena of much more momentous importance. One of my contentions is that the proliferation of large systems until they reach critical, unstable, and uneconomic dimensions will be followed by a breakdown at least as rapid as the previous expansion and will be accompanied by many catastrophic events. It follows that the two main features that will have to be recognized as symptoms of the arrival of the dark age will be a sharp diminution of population followed by a further, slower reduction, and a piecemeal breakup of large systems into many small, independent, and self-sufficient subsystems.

A decline in population was one of the features of the earlier dark age. Rome had over a million inhabitants in the imperial period, and only about 30,000 in the year 1100. This decline occurred throughout the Italian peninsula and the whole Mediterranean basin. Some historians see this as the cause rather than an effect of the Dark Ages—a debatable point of view. Others maintain that lowered productivity and the abandonment of agriculture were not due to a shrinkage of the absolute number of inhabitants in the Empire but to changes in the allocation of manual labor, and especially to the diminished availability of slave labor. It may be that the problem of determining the causes and effects of the fall of the Roman Empire is insoluble. In any case it is irrelevant to the forecasts that I am making, since today there is certainly no cause of regress that may be identified with a diminution of population: in almost every part of the world the population is increasing. And so, however things may have gone in the past, it is impossible that a sharp decrease in population in the future will be the prime cause of decline and fall: it will be the effect of regress and collapse produced by other causes.

If we postulate for the moment only that the population of the world will decline considerably in the course of a few years—say, by half—the obvious consequence will be a speedy glut of consumer goods, durable goods, and all industrial products, and they will quickly lose their value. A further result will be the interruption of research and invention, and the motives of profit and competition that are bound up with them. Even basic scientific research, though not interrupted, will slow down and go into the doldrums caused by the lack of advanced industrial products, organization, and finance.

This apocalyptic anticipation should not be used to search out other, facile parallels between the dark age that ended some centuries ago and the one now imminent. I shall not try, therefore, to guess what new migrations of peoples are likely—gratuitously identifying the Chinese of today with the Goths, Avars, and Huns of the past; nor shall I speculate about a revival of the religious spirit. My sole concern is to show that the ways in which large modern systems have been built up, and developed to excess, have to be analyzed if we are to understand the cause of their coming breakdown, of which there are numerous signs.

It would be trite to observe that the processes of unceasing growth and expansion pervading our world cannot go on indefinitely. Yet there is nothing trite, I think, about trying to foresee when we shall reach the knee, and what violent disturbances may occur in our passage from a variable order of things to one that will eventually be static. It would not be possible to examine, or even merely to enumerate, all the different kinds of processes by which our existing situation could degenerate into a standstill. As far as reason allows I must be content to develop the assumption already mentioned, of a single overshoot followed by an equally rapid shrinkage and decline, and to make its logical consequences explicit for the period that I have defined as the coming dark age.

The considerations that follow should not be treated as statistical extrapolations, the probability of their verification being assessed numerically. They are intuitions, based admittedly on the extrapolations of numerical evidence wherever it is relevant to the solution of the central problem, the breakdown of large systems.

Naturally the main interest in analyzing the causes of this breakdown would be to produce techniques, procedures, and organizational changes to prevent it. In the following chapters, devoted to particular problems in the various large systems, I shall ask what possibility of salvation exists for each, and try to show what measures are indispensable if the whole situation is not to degenerate inevitably into one of instability and chaos. Certain conclusions are obvious already: that is, that the necessary remedies are not being prepared, that simple remedies will not suffice, and that complicated remedies are not known. Trust in systems engineering will no longer do. The time is ripe to begin thinking constructively about setting up independent operational units to conserve our civilized know-how, so that this knowledge might survive the coming era of darkness and bring a new era to birth.

Is a Halt to Expansion Unlikely?

A good story going the rounds in business circles in the United States quotes the epitaph that Harold S. Geneen, volcanic president of International Telephone and Telegraph (ITT), is alleged to want on his tombstone: "Here lies the man who realized an annual 15 per cent increase in turnover for his corporation for very many years (the sequence is still unbroken), achieving at the same time a remarkable return on assets."

The second part of the epitaph is no less important than the first. In fact, it is much easier to increase turnover, accepting a diminution or a loss of profits, than to increase turnover, secure your profits in addition, and even increase them. And there is no doubt that even in an expanding economy Geneen's results are so exceptional that he is envied and emulated by presidents of corporations, large and small, throughout the United States.

The discussion in the previous chapter would suggest that Geneen's performance is even more remarkable, in view of the fact that growth is a phenomenon that be-

comes more and more unlikely. Recent economic and social history suggests that situations of equilibrium have a
duration in time which is percentually much longer than
situations of growth and development. Without getting
bogged down in the controversy about whether conditions
of static and uniform equilibrium have greater "natural-
ness," we can certainly affirm that there is small likelihood
nowadays that any man will succeed in causing manifold
growth in the organization that he has created or that
he is managing. Creators and expanders of industrial and
commercial empires were numerous in the last century,
but there will be few Geneens in the next hundred years.

My thesis, then, is that we shall soon have an oscillation,
with a jump to general levels somewhat higher than at
present; then a sharp swing downward to a minimum; and
at length a new growth at a moderate slope. I shall try to
show that the total range of the swing from the maximum
to the subsequent minimum position will be a few times
greater than the range of the cycles of prosperity and crisis
that have been the experience of the last hundred years.

This last fact gives dramatic quality to the events that I
am trying to foresee. To be more explicit, the dramas to
which I refer will consist of hecatombs of populations
much more momentous than those slaughters, irrelevant
by comparison, caused by wars, automobile accidents, and
epidemics. The drastic reduction in the density of people
on the earth will have profound consequences for every
form of human association, and many things that will be
new will be hardly bearable.

In view of this it is curious that there is a current of
contemporary thought which regards already as dramat-

ically dangerous some fairly marginal aspects of continuous expansion. As we shall see in Chapter IV, a research group at the Massachusetts Institute of Technology has shown that the increasing dimensions of large systems—but also the more basic facts of population explosion, increasing industrial production, increasing pollution, exhaustion of natural resources—cause instability in the situation of the entire planet. As a consequence serious crises are to be expected within a century. These are the predicaments that require continuous attention and huge efforts of both public and private powers. It is consequently inappropriate to focus attention on secondary consequences of increases in gross national products: yet there are so many voices loudly eloquent in their opposition and criticism of notorious side effects of growth that we have to consider their point of view carefully.

My own view that this preoccupation is mistaken is fairly obvious, even though I agree that many such criticisms are just, and even too timid. On the other hand, I should have little justification if—without citing sources—I presented a composite viewpoint reconstructed from several different writers, because then I would be setting up an ideal opponent so that I might be able to confute him more easily; therefore, I will cite extensively one of the most serious and articulate defenders of the point of view to which I have referred: E. J. Mishan, professor of economics at the London School of Economics, and in particular, his book *The Costs of Economic Growth*.[2] His arguments relevant to our discussion may be set out as follows:

1. Defined as *increase*—either of the gross national prod-

uct, or of average personal income, or of the average availability of durable consumer goods, or of average power consumption per head—economic growth should be considered desirable only insofar as it leads to a situation that is, in general, "optimal." An optimal situation is one in which no redistribution of the resources of society exists which would result in a higher total availability of goods valued at their market value. (In an optimal situation the market value of each good coincides with its marginal cost, marginal cost being defined as the quantity to be added to total cost in order to produce a further unit of the good under consideration.)

2. But this optimal concept should not be based on a consideration of market *prices*, since "external diseconomies" are inevitably involved in the production of every good. These diseconomies are defined as damages or losses that the production and use of certain goods may inflict on members of the public who may not be implicated in any way in the process of their production nor at all interested in their subsequent use.

3. It follows that the definition of the optimal situation has to be supplemented. The market value must be identified not with the sole marginal cost of production but with that cost supplemented by the value of the losses inflicted on the rest of society by the production and use of the goods in question. This total sum is defined as "social marginal cost."

Up to this point it is easy to agree with Professor Mishan, who observes acutely that the most probable reason why conventional economists and government statisticians fail to take account of the external diseconomies is that they involve imponderables that would be extremely difficult to measure precisely. Further, it is very difficult—whether you use some technique of measurement or some concept of value—to establish cause-and-effect relationships between each sector of the economy and each type of external diseconomy. One should not invoke these indubitable difficulties, however, to maintain that the external diseconomies are nonexistent or negligible.

So far so good. But Mishan's thesis goes on to list the things that seem to him most dangerous in an opulent and growing society; and here he becomes decidedly polemical. He commits himself, for example, to the statement: "The invention of the private automobile is one of the great disasters to have befallen the human race." His aversions are focused on the following situations.

4. The vast spread of private motoring: it chokes the channels of traffic and so destroys wealth; it pollutes the air; it spoils the proper enjoyment of natural and architectural beauty; it worsens both the character and the mind of the car driver during his long, slow progress in congested traffic; it sucks too large an amount of potential investment into the production of more and more vehicles, since the same resources could be used to produce more remunerative goods.

5. The excessive diffusion of air travel: it assaults all people living near airports with vexatious noise; it reduces the dimensions of our planet, making earth commonplace, less mysterious, and less interesting.

6. Mass tourism: it is responsible for the destruction of so much natural beauty, either through the tramplings of

tourists or through the spreading rash of artifacts to house, feed, move, and entertain them.

7. The cult of efficiency: it condemns too many people to a depersonalized and monotonous existence, preventing them from exploiting their own inventiveness and creativity, and from being independently productive as were master craftsmen of former times.

8. There are no isolated territorial reserves where all who abhor cars, transistor radios, and the noise of airplanes might gather and live a quieter life at a slower pace, enjoying the pleasures of family life and of genuine and profound human relationships such as existed in times past.

9. The excessive hold that advertisement and fashion have over the multitude: they create artificial needs which people are forced to satisfy by identifying themselves more completely with the economic process, and lowering their standard of taste.

10. The schemes and projects of engineers to deal with congestion by a profound change in basic structures. The Buchanan Report is typical. Drawn up by Professor Colin Buchanan in 1963 for the British Ministry of Transport, it proposes the restructure of cities with layout and architecture fitted to the needs of traffic. There would be, for example, a network of roads and buildings articulated at different levels so as to avoid crossroads and to ensure a continuous flow of unimpeded traffic. But the solution preferred by Mishan is to leave the cities as they are, to abolish all private traffic, and to invest huge sums in improving public (collective) transportation.

It is clear that in theses 4 to 10, as I have enumerated

them, there is a serious infiltration of ideology; and Mishan admits this without reserve. In setting out my objections I shall try to keep ideological controversy to a minimum and to rely chiefly on quantitative considerations. These will be meant to show that the evils cited by Mishan are grave, but not so much in themselves as in the fact that they represent symptoms of a tendency toward something far more grave, i.e., an intrinsic instability and a total congestion, from which could follow what I have called the new dark age.

With reference to theses 4 and 10 one should remember that there are endless debates between experts on traffic and transportation, many of whom would like to see public transportation eliminated altogether (as in many parts of the United States), whereas others would like it clearly favored, with reserved lanes in which to operate, the prohibition of private parking, etc. And here it should be added that in all cities where traffic conditions are worsening through traffic congestion, a disproportionate area of road surface is used for parking stationary vehicles, and there is no modern and efficient system for controlling and regulating traffic. In cities where off-street parking has been made possible by building underground or multi-storied garages, the situation is much better, and the existing urban road network is able to satisfy traffic demands. The city of Madrid is a good example. There off-street parking facilities for 25,000 cars are already in operation, and accommodations for an equal number are being built. In Rome and New York there are no initiatives of this kind on a comparable scale, and the situation is worse. Electronic methods of fixed timing for the automatic regulation of urban traffic could help to enlarge the traffic capacity of existing streets and thus increase the average speed of vehicles by 20 per cent or more: this would get rid of the worst congestions.

It is true that large systems for the electronic regulation of urban traffic have not always been successful in making it flow more easily. There are well-known cases where such attempts have been complete failures, inspiring an emphatic disbelief that the notorious problems of road traffic can possibly be solved by electronic devices. We should note, however, that the worst failures have happened when a low-level type of systems engineering was used, and there was an unjustifiable assumption that to employ a very large digital computer would guarantee success. As we shall see, things do not work so simply; nor is it reasonable to conclude that any possible technological solution must be inadequate solely because so many of them to which people have had recourse have proved singularly inefficient, and even harmful. Generally speaking, many technical system solutions—the success of which should be certain by present-day standards—have often been operated from the start in a foolishly third-rate way: this is another fact inducing pessimistic doubt about whether the large systems in the most advanced nations can possibly reach a state of equilibrium without being badly shaken in the process.

As for point 5, we may note briefly that recent psychological research seems to show that the noise made by airplanes is not such a grievous scourge, since the work that people do is not appreciably (and therefore adversely) affected by the degree of noise to which they are subjected. And here again, congestion rather than noise is the much graver problem—congested air traffic, whether in the air or on the ground at airports. The arguments already used with reference to vehicle traffic in cities are precisely applicable here too; and there is the further consideration that the *speed* of modern air transport produces external economies (rather than diseconomies), eliminating much immobilization in the handling of goods and so contributing an asset to the economic balance of air transport.

Point 6 contains faulty reasoning. Any prevention of mass tourism—whether through regulations or by imposing artificial and additional economic burdens—would imply that the beauties of nature may be saved from the deterioration caused by crowds if they are reserved for a few. But the choosing of those few is not a task that could be discharged fairly. The dilemma becomes even more awkward if we try to show that the presence of crowds always leads to an irremediable ruin of nature's amenities, for no such demonstration is possible. Evidence to the contrary is available and convincing. There are successful regulations for preserving the landscape and special environments. If there is a problem here, it is not so very serious, since there is only one inhabitant to every $12\frac{1}{2}$ acres of land on the surface of the globe. But it will become a very serious problem indeed if the population density of the world continues to grow at its present rate; for this will mean a much more than proportional increase of population density in the great storehouses of humanity, the huge agglomerations of people in cities. This is the critical and fearsome situation that really matters, since it can lead to unstable equilibrium and the grave phenomena of collapse long before the secondary effects of tourism would justify anxiety.

My objection to point 7—the criticism of the cult of efficiency—is that I deny the facts alleged to support it. We know that scientists now living outnumber all their predecessors since the beginning of history. In strictly numerical terms, then, there has never been an epoch such as ours in which so many people have obtained such massive gratification from the exploitation of their own inventiveness and creativity. This is true, incidentally, even if we discount the fact that the intellectual and professional level of most living scientists is much lower than it is generally believed to be. Even if we think in terms of percentages, this conclusion is unaffected. In fact there is no sense in comparing the conditions of life enjoyed by the better-class artisans of any past century with those of the less specialized workers who are employed in the big automated factories of today. A reference to the United States shows that in 1850 the percentage of the active population employed in agriculture was 65 per cent. In 1900 it was 38 per cent, and today it is less than 12 per cent. Taking into account the percentage of the working population employed in "tertiary" activities such as services, the transportation and distribution of goods, etc., it is clear that even 120 years ago skilled artisans represented but a meager minority of the population. The most significant movement, therefore, has been from agriculture to industry and—by now—from agriculture to services. Since 1956 the number of people in the United States employed in tertiary activities has exceeded the number of people employed in the productive activities of both industry and agriculture. And here it is only those who know the agricultural environment firsthand who are really aware that the activities pursued by peasants in a fairly primitive economy were and are more monotonous and brutalizing than those that are typical of workers in modern industry. The alleged amenities permitted by the slower rhythms of rural life often coincide with an inescapably sluggish and deprived existence. Those precious human relationships that the life of a rural peasantry is supposed to foster have to rest in fact on a basis of absolute cultural poverty: they become stereotyped, exchanging the same unvarying verbal formulas. Decades of such standardization have codified even their forms of humor.

I cannot doubt that the greater availability of information today—the wider range of choices now open to people, enabling them to reach a higher cultural and professional level—is a positive element in any vision of the world that affirms the primacy of human values over monetary values.

The ideas summarized in points 8 and 9 affirm the desirability of separate territorial reserves where there would be no mechanization of any kind, and where all the discomforts deriving from the technical equipment of modern life would be avoided—noise, pollution, nervous strain, etc. This experiment has already been tried—certain communities of Mennonites have been in existence in Pennsylvania for some time now. They do not allow their members to possess or to make use of the automobile, radio, television, telephone, telegraph, of cameras, movies, alcohol, or tobacco. Though these conditions coincide with what seems desirable to people who loathe the stress of modern existence, these communities have no striking recruitment, even though they have attracted a certain publicity in the press and in film documentaries. One must assume that other similar protective refuges would be favored by relatively few people.

It is here that we ought to consider the familiar question, revived by Mishan, of how good taste is to be defined and how it is to be influenced and molded. I think that all attempts at establishing an official good taste lead inevitably to hateful impositions and persecutions. Soviet society furnishes some examples. Quite apart from controversy over socialist realism or Stalinist interpretations of art, it is interesting to notice that the latest tendency in the land of collective transport (duly justified by ideology) seems to be toward an increase in private transportation.

It is understandable that certain manifestations of a uniform undeveloped taste may triumph; and it is reasonable that individual reactions to this must be personal. All classifications of good taste inevitably contain statistical elements, and references to groups with predilections for certain forms rather than others. Objective judgments delivered *a priori* are obviously meaningless. For example, in Pakistan certain types of music are played only in the morning and it would be bad taste to play them in the evenings. To call this custom ridiculous has no more sense *sub specie aeternitatis* than to mock pop music or football.

The inconveniences and discomforts of society in the advanced nations of today may be greater than those that prevailed in the past: we have already noticed that it is an arguable issue. But such discomforts are of negligible importance when compared with the final abyss. Anyone who is too preoccupied with them is—to use appropriate apocalyptic vividness—like a prisoner in a crowded, locked freight car who complains about the uncomfortable ride and gives no thought to the extermination camp that awaits him.

▌▌▌

Large Systems and Their Engineering

Before describing any actual cases of deterioration and breakdown in large systems, and anticipating others in the future that will be worse, we must define what is meant by "large system," giving some account of how such systems are designed.

Without aiming at a strictly scientific definition, I mean by "large system" any organization whose functions involve the following factors: an adequately large number of people participating in it as operators or users; certain procedures, either actually or potentially formalized; and the use of machinery or apparatus whereby all these elements contribute specific means for the attainment of a definite end.

The great Egyptian pyramids provide an ancient example. The organized planning, designing, and building of them—by manpower and by various technical devices—was certainly a large system. And in our own time the thrust of modern expansion and growth has meant the proliferation of huge systems, such as:

• systems of communication, by telephone, telegraph, or telex, covering a nation or a continent

• railway systems, comprising stations, track, rolling stock, with subsystems for signaling and safety, ticketing and reservation, railway personnel and traveling public— and auxiliary services

• airlines, and systems for the control of air traffic

• systems for the regulation, control, and supervision of vehicular traffic on streets, roads, and highways

• systems generating, transmitting, and distributing electrical energy

• postal systems

• industrial processes of mechanized production

• military defense systems, comprising surveillance, early warning radar systems, electronic counter-measures, interception

This list is far from being exhaustive, and is drawn up in very general terms.

Many of these systems were built up without any long-term planning on the part of their designers: they were gradually modified to meet growing demands as problems of increasing magnitude arose. Often such adaptations have had no more than moderate success.

Though it doubtless happens that systems engineers are called in to start from scratch and to plan systems that are entirely new, their work consists much more often of restructuring existing systems known to be inadequate, or of bringing them up to date so that they may give better service. They explore the possibilities of automation, which may depend on whether apparatus for measurement and electronic control is available—particularly electronic computers able to exercise many functions of data processing, decision, and control traditionally entrusted to human operators.

A characteristic common to almost all large systems is their striking complexity. Designing (or redesigning) a system, therefore, requires an accurate analysis of its institutional purpose, its structure, and the flow of information within it. This analysis in turn requires that the aims of the system be redefined in a formal way by means of a mathematical model; that is, a complex of mathematical formulas, procedures, or charts that enable one to foresee how the system will behave without actually setting it going. Not that the model is thought of as "determinist": as it has to reckon with real situations it will incorporate numerous probabilities, especially when the elements of its problem are inevitably numerous. For example, when a telephone network is to be designed, there is no way of knowing beforehand how many of the future subscribers will want to be making a call or will actually be telephoning at any given moment in the future; the only thing to do is to estimate various alternatives on the basis of probability theory, and to translate design into actuality in such a way that the consequences of each foreseen alternative may be acceptable.

When complicated facts are schematized as formal mathematical relations, it often happens that their description as furnished by formulas is not quite accurate, and as the accuracy of the model is only approximate, it follows that forecasts based solely upon it may be equally inaccurate. Its validity has to be confirmed, therefore, in order to discover whether it can be profitably used; and if so, how far. To this end experiments are planned, so that their results (already assessed by the model) may be checked in practice, and the difference between estimated and effective measurement determined.

All this defines what the system has to do and provides the mathematical language for discussing with precision subsequent steps. The next step is to define the logic of the system: that is, to decide what must happen to each of its elements in each of the situations in which it may find itself during its (spatial or temporal) passage through the process. This stage of the whole project is known as "single-thread design." It does not yet aim at deciding on technical solutions, or types of equipment, or on how the people who will eventually make it all work are to be organized. It aims only at stating the functions that a given element has to meet from the moment it enters the system to the moment it leaves it.

After deciding just what we want to happen in every possible circumstance to each phone call, to each train, to each airplane, or to each posted letter—details preordained and controlled by the system—we have to reckon with the fact that the number of these elements to be found simultaneously within the system at any one time is generally very high. That is, we are concerned here with crowded systems, of high density. Very rarely, therefore, can the single-thread design completely solve all the individual problems that may present themselves. It cannot resolve the problems of incompatibility that arise when two or more elements simultaneously demand the fulfillment of a function of the system; the system is limited, and depends on what the available plant and services can manage to do. Put more generally, the system has to be planned for conditions of heavy traffic. It must be able to function even when congestion occurs, so long as that congestion is contained within reasonable limits. What does "reasonable" mean here? Though this is a very delicate and debatable question, there must certainly be such limits; otherwise the system becomes too complicated and costly to put into practice.

Telephone systems illustrate this problem well. Because telephone calls are confidential, and crosstalk is obviously to be avoided, it is an accepted principle that no subscriber may be put through to another already engaged in conversation with someone else. Now, it would be possible, apart from this limiting case, to avoid all forms of telephone congestion simply by installing enough lines to connect all the subscribers, two by two, in all possible combinations. ("Congestion" is defined here as a situation in which subscriber X fails to get through to subscriber Y, who is free, because the existing lines are already engaged by subscribers other than X and Y.) But this would mean constructing a telephone system at an unacceptably high cost, and no telephone company has ever even considered it. Five billion lines would be necessary to connect 100,000 subscribers, two by two, in all possible ways. And so, apart from the fact that there are satisfactory techniques for reducing the number of telephone lines, normally the networks are so planned that approximately 20 per cent of all the subscribers can make calls at the same time. In spite of this limitation, the delays imposed on callers in well-designed networks are very brief; and the cases in which a call cannot be completed for a very long time are fairly rare. And yet it is true that the entire telephone system of the United States would be blocked if 25 million Americans should decide to use the phone simultaneously.

Designers of systems normally act on the principle that it is as inadvisable as it is costly to have a structure that only satisfies demand where probability is very low. They consider a system good enough if it functions satisfactorily on 364 days in the year, even though for one day a year, on average, its service is inadequate.

There are real dangers, however. Congestion may have been negligibly low when the system was first designed, but if it should grow, there will be complications. This is precisely what happens when there is economic expansion, population explosion, and improvement in average living conditions. The services of the system then become chronically insufficient because they have to function amid conditions of intense activity; congestion becomes almost continuous, and the majority of consumers get service that is poor and unsatisfactory.

The very existence of certain systems—normally in the military field—is due to competitive conflict situations. The people involved in the system's operation may, then, be separated into two groups such that any advantage obtained by one group produces a certain disadvantage for the other group. Situations of this type may be studied analytically, applying the well-known theories of mathematical games. However, these theories are actually useful only in well-defined and fairly simple cases in which enough information is available concerning the probability of certain events and the advantages or disadvantages implied by them.

The mathematical theory of games may also be applied when a conflict of interest exists, such as when cheating (or avoiding payment) is advantageous to a system user. The system designer will then have to evaluate the probability of cheating, measure the loss, and compare the disadvantage to the organization which runs or owns the system against the cost of the procedures or safety systems necessary to avoid frauds or to detect cheating.

The function of the system being defined, we come to its structure and to a particular problem—whether to centralize or decentralize: that is, whether the system works to greater advantage as one large central establishment or as many specialized establishments located even at some distance from one another. The former solution is clearly preferable if the system has a limited regional extension, and also if the functions to be discharged by the equipment are highly complicated—mathematical calculations, for example; for this would necessitate the use of machines with a very high processing capacity and would justify investing in a single central computer of high performance. But if the places producing the data for processing are distant from one another (separate branches of banks, for example), communication between the several sources of data and the processing center is much more costly. Yet here again centralization has recently become easier, since inexpensive terminals are now available giving two-way communication with the large central electronic computer. On the other hand, the decentralized solution is preferable whenever the requisite processing of data is sufficiently simple; for then it turns out that several similar machines doing identical jobs at the circumference are less expensive, since they bring down the cost of channeling information to the center.

In these systems a twofold flow is discernible. The main one is the flow of objects that the system is designed to handle: men, vehicles, goods, power, messages, etc. The other is the control flow consisting of signals, produced automatically or by hand, which transmit relevant information from the world outside to the system's units or its control center. The control flow also includes processed signals, represented by symbols, feeding decisions from the center to the action points where machines or men put them into practice. Further, it includes signals representing information on which no action has necessarily to be taken; this is sent out so that the operating personnel may be aware of what is happening at any moment, spot any irregularity that may occur, and intervene directly overriding normal control procedure.

The final stage of so-called technological implementation is realized as designers define the performance and characteristics of their total apparatus—for making calculations, transmitting information, processing data, controlling peripheral units, and carrying out decisions. In some cases it is necessary to design and build special instruments and apparatus having the sole aim of satisfying the operational needs of the system. In other cases, instruments and apparatus already designed for other purposes are incorporated into the system; and sometimes it actually happens that certain available machines or technological means provide the initial idea for the aim and structure of the system, or at least have a marked influence upon it.

Every system should satisfy the aims for which it was designed and built; but such a statement is vague and useless as it stands. Every system should be defined precisely by some numerical measure of its efficiency and worth which will indicate how well it is doing—how far it is succeeding in achieving its ends. But is there a coefficient of success here that is physically appreciable and quantitatively measurable? Can the worth of a system be estimated as a percentage achievement of some ideal optimum? It is tempting to think so. But though the efficiency of machines turning thermal energy into mechanical energy is precisely definable, there is hardly ever a comparable yardstick for assessing the performance of large complex systems. They do not satisfy the simple linear features proper to a good measure of effectiveness, because they rarely lend themselves to such quantitative measurement. It is equally tempting, of course, to rely on intuitive evaluations, based not on weights and measures but on direct experience of the system's working, or of some particular aspect of it: you have a hunch that may or may not be authentic.

It is clear from the foregoing definitions that many of the large systems are not intended to obtain one type of result having to do with one class of objects only. They may have multiple aims corresponding respectively to the various categories of consumers and objects making up the system. And there is no easy way to decide which may be the better of two alternative solutions when one of them offers a better performance in one part of the whole system, but a worse one in another part of it. There are mathematical techniques for putting such different solutions in order of preference; but their use may lead to conclusions in mathematical form too difficult for those who have to make the final decision—often people who are administrators rather than experts in operations research.

There is a further necessity. Criteria should be available by which to evaluate the system on the basis of current results. A process of feedback is needed that will allow the mathematical models to be refined and statistics to be improved and that will submit to approximate revision the very specifications of the system: that is, its logical requirements and even the individual functions and characteristics of its various parts, and the equipment that it is using.

Despite the great difficulty of evaluating systems by using numbers to indicate their respective degrees of merit, it is fashionable nowadays for those who design systems and those who sell them to claim that they have reached perfection and are first-class. But it is very rare that such claims to excellence are clearly demonstrated. Often they are propaganda boosting the system in question.

Here we have to remember that in every problem to which systems give rise, the number of variables to be considered is very great, and the number of their different combinations—or of the decisions about the way in which each of them may be treated—is enormous. (This is so, quite apart from the difficulty of comparing performance, actual or designed, with some indefinably perfect or ideal performance satisfying the requirements of the system

100 per cent.) Since to very many combinations of variables or of decisions there correspond just as many possible alternative solutions, one could not pronounce judicially that this or that solution is the best one without having examined the technical setup and the implications (performance, relation of cost to benefits, operational safety, probable life) of *all* the solutions. Only by such a procedure—so long and costly as to be prohibitive—would one have enough data to pronounce this or that solution as effectively the best from all points of view. That procedure would also be excluded by the practical consideration that a system that has taken but a short time to become operative, and is only just satisfactory, is often preferable to a much better one arrived at after a much longer period, and after having cost much more to design.

H. Raiffa and R. Schlaiffer have argued convincingly that for the ends in view it would be an advantage deliberately to renounce "optimizing" for "satisfying" criteria: and in fact what happens in practice in the initial stages of designing a system (and some designers seem to be ashamed of it) is that certain basic decisions are made in a way that is largely intuitive; whole classes of possible solutions are discarded, and analytical evaluation renounced; only after the structure of the system in its main lines has been settled does one go on to a formal analysis of the few alternatives that remain.

We shall be noticing later that systems engineering is at present going through a time of crisis, not only because of the difficulties already discussed but because others much more commonplace abound. Those difficulties may summarize thus:

1. Many engineers, managers, administrators, and government officials do not suspect that problems even exist in this field. They suppose that any critical situation can be dealt with by means of ad hoc action, special artifacts or machinery: that is, technical or handbook solutions each conceived to provide a particular service or to remedy some single trouble. An executive rarely imagines that his requirements for the solution of one problem may actually contradict those that he has prescribed for solving the problem next door to it; yet this type of thing happens frequently.

2. Even when a handbook solution would indeed solve some isolated problem, no use is made of it, thanks to inertia, neglect, or lack of interest.

3. Estimates of future developments in critical situations are often not even attempted; and in those exceptional cases where such an attempt is made, it is limited to modest linear extrapolations; there is no imaginative effort that might allow a man to discern the drastically new shape of things at hand—elements completely different from those already known. The result is that many systems come to birth old and antiquated. "I conclude then," says Machiavelli,[3] "that since fortune varies and since men remain fixed in their ways, men are successful as long as these ways conform to each other, but unsuccessful when they are opposed to each other."

4. Many designers of systems divide the main problem into subsidiary problems, each of which is resolvable by relatively simple methods based on linear hypotheses: that is, the simple apportioning of effects to causes. They relegate all questions about the integrated and simultaneous

operation of these various facts to the so-called interface, i.e., equipment for intercommunication and adaptation. In this way the design of the interface often gets less attention than that given to the subsidiary problems, probably because of its difficulty.

5. Many who administer systems overrate the importance of their documentation procedures. These are meant to record and check the specifications, the design, the variations, and the progress of the system that is being worked out. But the means become the end, and the world of paper is mistaken for the real world. Some even ignore the existence of the real world and regard their paper work as alone true and important. In this way systems are realized that function coherently on paper but are divorced from reality and are largely useless. This particular situation is more general than my brief reference to it may suggest. It has deep roots in the tradition of mismanagement, which is one of the remote causes of the imminent world crisis. We must examine it more closely in what follows.

IV

Large Systems Getting Out of Control

In his book *Culture and History* (1958) Philip Bagby wrote that the size of a culture—i.e., the number of people sharing actively in it—seems to be in itself a fact of little significance, though naturally the political and economic organization of large areas implies problems somewhat different from those of small areas.

It would be surprising that one of the most discerning of those modern scientists attempting a logico-experimental analysis of history and civilization should have expressed himself so oversimply about so grave a question, were it not that the majority of planners, technicians, systems engineers, and politicians today are still guilty of underrating the consequences implied by the size of the huge agglomerations of modern men.

For years, however, we have had a tragic problem of congestion in the large systems, centered as they are in the world's greater urban areas, their effective signs being the ceaseless flux of people, vehicles, goods, electric power, communications, and waste products. It is a problem that grows continually worse. Even the less informed public complains of daily traffic congestion in city streets, on interurban roads, and in the air; of the inadequacy and unreliability of the networks for transmitting and distributing power; of the untrustworthiness and insufficiency of the communication networks. All this disturbs and disquiets multitudes of people. It is noteworthy too that it destroys wealth.

The figures involved are enormous, but unfortunately no precise and complete evaluations of them are available. Systematic analyses in this field are an urgent necessity. Here, however, are certain data by way of example.

The U.S. Federal Aviation Agency estimated in 1969 that the lack of adequate airports and airport facilities in the city of New York alone will result in an annual loss to the city's economy of $200 million a year by 1975 and of $650 million by 1980.

The Italian Ministry of Public Works estimates that road traffic congestion involves the Italian public in an annual loss of from $1,600 to 3,200 million; the very vagueness of this estimate does not even try to hide how shaky and unreliable is the process whereby this official body acquires its data.

Experts in various fields are often able to specify single inadequacies that are largely responsible for many of these unsatisfactory aspects of urban life; and it is often true that technical instruments and pieces of apparatus now available could much improve the situation if employed on a large scale. But, in fact, they are often used only sporadically and sometimes not at all. For example, the U.S. Air Force has made large and very advantageous use of three-dimensional radar, but the Federal Aviation Agency has ruled that the equipment is not accurate enough for use in commercial aviation.

Then there is the ever-increasing difficulty of controlling city traffic. Planners often reach the decision—frequently unjustified—that their budgets prevent them from solving congestion problems with impressive works of civil engineering, such as intersections operating at two or three levels by means of overpass and underpass, and off-street parking for stationary vehicles so that the entire street area may be reserved for moving vehicles alone. The reasonable cheaper alternative, then, is control by means of traffic lights. But once this decision is taken, too often it means renouncing a long-term advantage: it means giving up the chance of using electronic controls with their time gaps varying as the flow of traffic requires, and using instead the fixed time gaps of electric mechanisms which are not always reliable. In this way cities renounce using existing structures at maximum efficiency, and using their antiquated street networks satisfactorily.

Some instructive case histories have been collected by Roger K. Field under the significant title "Urban Hardware Grounds the Aerospace Experts."[4] Field's work documents the crying metropolitan needs in communications, road and rail traffic control, adequate systems for water supply and waste disposal, the control of atmospheric pollution—problems that some of the major corporations, already successful in aerospace programs, have tried to solve without success.

At this point we should note that indiscriminate decisions to use digital electronic computers to solve any problem in the operation or control of complex systems actually beg the question in that such decisions assume the unlimited flexibility of computers. But before there is any recourse to such machines, the procedures of operation and control have to be formally and fully defined: in other words, operational problems have to be satisfactorily solved apart from what technology may later add.

The use of inadequate or unsuitable equipment certainly contributes to the problems of megalopolis, and this is a challenge to the more advanced electronic industries. Yet it is not by accepting this challenge and even winning notable successes that the problems may be properly tackled and solved. For there are two kinds of defects at the system level that cannot be remedied simply by inventing special technical hardware.

The first might be labeled "miscalculation." A thoroughly sound theory is misapplied numerically, either through incompetence or because there is a sudden and unexpected increase in the size and complexity of the system. Take, for example, the theory of static and dynamic stability in the transmission networks of electric power, which was stated classically by S. B. Crary. This theory was available—but it did not help—when the blackout suddenly hit the entire northeast United States in November 1965. The crisis was immediate because the parameters for the operating thresholds of the circuit breakers had been wrongly selected and the differential safeguarding devices wrongly staggered. Another example is the theory of congestion in telephone networks: it has not enabled New York or Paris to avoid serious paralysis in telephone systems. Forecasts of future increases in consumers' demands have proved to be far too timid and conservative. There are rational and unambiguous ways of remedying this type of defect without having to invent anything radically new.

The second type of defect is evident when a system lacks theoretical concepts and mathematical models able to represent the real world and to make forecasts of its future developments. This applies to huge megalopolitan concentrations of people considered (as they certainly should be) as single systems. It applies, also, to some subsystems that are part of a megalopolitan system; and to the interaction of two or more of them—particularly when one of them is suddenly overloaded, thanks to some random swing in consumers' preference. We lack the basic theory (and even the terminology) for handling such events. For example, although models of vehicular traffic in vast urban areas have been devised and sometimes used, there is no theory about them yet in existence that has reached a completeness comparable to that of statistical theories on the function and usage of telephone networks. And when theory is lacking, no sensible forecast can be made of the time necessary to verify it. This is confirmed when we note that attempts at progress are too often made in casually chosen directions, the result being a speed of progress that is very low (apparently proportional to the square root of the time spent on research).

If all the advantages available from textbook solutions were actually obtained, many things would improve accordingly, and the threatening crisis (which many signs persuade us is imminent) would be less tragic; even though it may be unavoidable, it would at least be postponed. The destruction of wealth, the frustrations and hardships caused by it, are not in fact the worst evils. Crowded cities create a close interdependence between all the large systems that converge there; each of these systems may sometimes vicariously assume functions that are normally discharged by one of the others (use of the telephone when the postal system is not functioning; resort to personal movement when both telephone and postal system fail). Thus the worst evil is easily recognized: the breakdown of many large systems in the same area at the same time.

To show how deadly the consequences of several coincident breakdowns could be, let us look at certain phenomena of congestion that have occurred in recent years in one of the areas of the world that is highly advanced, technologically speaking, but in which the world's largest systems are also concentrated. I mean the northeastern coast of the United States.

On November 9, 1965, the interconnected network carrying electrical power throughout New England, New York, and Ontario, Canada, became unstable and there was no electricity for periods of up to fourteen hours in an area occupied by 30 million people. This meant the sudden absence of some 40,000 megawatts of power. In New York City alone 600,000 people were marooned in the subways. The movement of the inhabitants was further limited by the fact that no vehicles could refuel, because the electric motors of oil pumps were out of action.

On January 9, 1970, an accumulation of chance circumstances caused a breakdown of normal service on the Penn Central railway system (which serves, among others, the cities of New York and Philadelphia). Out of a normal total of 413 trains, 117 did not run at all, and 290 of the 296 that did run suffered serious delays.

In the autumn of 1969 an unexpected increase in the demand for service in the New York telephone network was accompanied by a worsening of its maintenance service. The result was the almost total stoppage of one of the automatic switchboards. For several consecutive days it was virtually impossible to obtain a free line on the affected part of the network, and for months afterward subscribers in the entire New York area had to endure long delays, and often to abandon the use of the telephone altogether.

Traffic jams that paralyze road transport are everyday experiences, too familiar to need mentioning.

But let us now imagine a situation in which all the crises just mentioned happen at the same time, and when weather conditions are bad: heavy snow, for example, and the temperature well below zero. It can be argued of course that the probability of such a concomitance of chance events is extraordinarily small; yet it is equally obvious that the hypothesis is not invalid, and that the huge and unprecedented catastrophe that it implies is not impossible. Indeed, the effects of different single crises would not add up to one total, as in simple arithmetic; they would amplify one another. Millions of people would die of cold and hunger for reasons and in ways that I shall describe later in greater detail.

The congestion of urban systems now takes place at much higher absolute levels and in greater density than in the past because modern technology allows a somewhat fuller exploitation of the resources and space available. Mathematical theories are being elaborated to define when the levels of congestion become critical and to determine the limits beyond which the dimensions of an urban system should not be allowed to go. These limits depend on the number, size, and type of the available channels of interchange; also on the number, quality, and efficiency of the technical means used to reduce the "impedance" or hindrance that the channels oppose to what is flowing through them.

History confirms what calculations indicate—that 2 million inhabitants was the maximum capacity of an ancient city where only pedestrians and vehicles drawn by animals circulated. It is a matter of opinion what the actual limits of population density are today, imposed as they are by the mobility of modern means of transport and by the degree of efficiency with which they are used. Although a theoretical limit of 40 million inhabitants has been suggested for a modern city, no city has yet passed the 20 million mark. But whether or not a city larger than that could possibly remain stable, present rates of development are tending to levels that are definitely higher and less stable, and from which a sharp plunge to very low levels is no impossibility. The vast city populations that will first exceed 20 million will be New York City with the densely populated areas of New Jersey, and the total population of Tokyo and Yokohama, which is already approaching 16 million.

I have mentioned the inefficiency typical of the Penn Central railway system. The company owning it went bankrupt at the beginning of the summer of 1970. The deeper causes of the failure have doubtless to be sought in disorganization: freight cars simply lost; trains ready to leave but unable to do so for lack of locomotives; freight trains made up with not more than seventy-five cars on transcontinental routes, solely to avoid having another brakeman on the train while crossing Indiana, as prescribed by the regulations of that state. But the more obvious causes of the financial failure may be identified as mistaken management decisions. In the last five years the company began to diversify its activities; about $150 million was invested in real estate companies in hopes of making percentage profits at least double those yielded by the railway, which were from 2 to 3 per cent. At first this seemed ingenious, but due to the recession of the American economy and to crashes on Wall Street, these speculations in real estate led to heavy losses which only added to the losses being incurred by the railway (a loss of $56 million in 1969; an average loss of $640,000 a day in 1970). Bankruptcy became inevitable.

Since 1970 the trustees of Penn Central have been making attempts at reorganization—but in vain. The February 17, 1973, issue of *Business Week* reports that "Congress has committed the federal government to finding a solution to the deepening Penn Central mess." The predicament is as follows. Half of the 20,000-mile trackage of the Penn Central has a high traffic density and is profitable; the second half eats up all the profits from the first and causes such heavy losses that the giant railroad will have to face liquidation by court order, unless at least 5,000 miles of seldom-used track are abandoned or unless the Administration provides a subsidy of at least $600 million —to start with. On the other hand "the Penn Central is vital to the economy," as its service is essential both for industrial giants—such as General Motors, Ford, and Bethlehem Steel—and for smaller companies throughout Pennsylvania.

Pennsylvania's governor, Milton J. Shapp, stated that the liquidation of Penn Central would ruin the economy of the East.

The problem is clearly one of size: the Penn Central is considered to be about twice as big as it ought to be. The move made in 1968 to merge the Pennsylvania and New York Central lines may well have been the remote cause of the subsequent collapse, although we can only guess whether the two railroads combined as Penn Central would be in better shape had they each remained independent. I have gone into this in detail only to show how a breakdown in the system can be hastened as a result of business and financial mismanagement.

In general, the crises occurring in the twentieth century that are due, like the crisis of 1929, to economic causes, seem even graver than those caused by war. Economic systems show a cyclic behavior of varying period and amplitude, and the government officials, financiers, and bankers who run them have—like most of us—very vague ideas of how and why these cycles occur. It was the claim of Clement Juglar that he had found their cycle periods to be from seven to nine years, whereas Joseph Kitchin maintained that it lasted forty months from one boom to the next; and N. D. Kondratieff assumed that he had correctly established their duration as forty-five years. These interpretations of certain regularities discernible in the economic phenomena of the past hardly allow us to foresee the economic future with any certainty. If such foresight were possible, more effective precautions against inflation or recession could be taken; and comparing stock exchanges with games of chance at a casino would not be justified.

The fact is that this ultimate economic ignorance and this inability to control economic systems are evidence of something more general: while the size and complexity of large systems tend to outgrow any level once regarded as their upper limit, our ability to control and direct them is not growing but deteriorating, and showing itself to be more and more inadequate.

One of the more interesting contributions to our understanding of the dynamic behavior of industrial, urban, and world-wide systems has recently been made by Professor Jay W. Forrester, of the Massachusetts Institute of Technology. Tackling the phenomena of transition—whether from growth to equilibrium or from growth to stagnation—he uses mathematical models (handled on digital computers) to study the varying levels reached by a system and the varying rates at which they are reached. It is a method of analysis used in automatic feedback control systems. Forrester makes the penetrating point that solutions to these complex problems cannot be arrived at intuitively, or by assuming simple cause-and-effect relationships between relevant factors in pairs. The existence of multiple feedback loops shows just how complex adequate solutions are; in actual fact they are "counterintuitive." A key concept in his more recent book *World Dynamics*[5] is interaction. Forrester examines the interactions of natural resources, capital investment, pollution, population, and "quality of life." This latter, for example, is conditioned by interacting realities—material standard of living, food supply, crowding, and pollution. He concludes that within the next century the population may drop dramatically and rapidly because of the interaction of factors just mentioned, and because planned intervention unwisely directed at reaching equilibrium may be self-defeating. Forrester does not consider the possibility that is the theme of this book: namely, that a dark age is imminent because of the coming breakdown of large technological systems, and that its arrival and dominance could happen in a matter of weeks or months rather than of decades. But there can be no doubt that the type of analysis that he is advocating will do much to clarify and to "quantify" the phenomena I am discussing.

During the early months of 1972, scientists from the Massachusetts Institute of Technology contributed a study entitled *The Limits to Growth* under the sponsorship of the Club of Rome's project on the predicament of mankind. It gave further currency to the general hypothesis of a coming collapse; and, along with its mathematical analyses based on Forrester's ideas, it received wide notoriety. This study examines several hypotheses to which present world trends have given rise and gives broad support to their common conclusion that the system of the civilized world as we know it will break down before very long (its population falling tragically to levels lower than those of today) if its unordered development continues without informed planning. The fundamental causes of the crisis would be: (1) industrial: the available deposits of raw materials in the world are being exhausted; (2)

agricultural: the mechanization of agriculture cannot go on increasing at its present pace, nor will agricultural production suffice to satisfy the hunger of the world; (3) environmental: among the direct results of increasing pollution is an increase in mortality. Even if we make a threefold assumption—that new deposits of raw materials may be discovered to replace those now approaching exhaustion; that there can be far more reuse of materials now jettisoned as waste; that pollution can and will be drastically reduced—crisis and breakdown will still be unavoidable, and for two main reasons: (a) the population explosion involves a large and unceasing increase in the extension of human settlements that will rob the cultivable surface of the earth still further and (b) increasing industrial production worsens the total problem of pollution even though reforms reduce some of its local and individual offenses.

Equilibrium is possible (rather than instability and collapse), but only if

• world population is stabilized, the birth rate being kept identical with the death rate

• industrial production is restricted, so that pollution is contained, and the excessive exploitation of the earth's natural resources stopped

• industrial waste products are made subject to drastic purifying processes until their noxious effects are reduced to one quarter of what they are now

• conservation becomes a reality, through the reuse of scrap, etc., rather than the rejection of it as expendable, and through conservation of the soil from exploitation and erosion.

Controversy has raged over *The Limits to Growth*. A superficial and derogatory review was published by *The Economist* in March 1972 and John Maddox voiced the opinion that the study is a nonsensical manifestation of the "Doomsday Syndrome." A positive endorsement was given by Sicco Mansholt. A good omen may be represented by the fact that Forrester's approach is currently inspiring a number of interesting studies of socioeconomic phenomena, which appear for example in the *Transactions on Systems, Man and Cybernetics* of the Institute of Electrical and Electronics Engineers.

It is sad that Forrester's approach is not likely to be accepted as congenial by those in charge of large systems. In the meantime large systems are becoming more and more unmanageable. Nobody knows how to make and keep them stable, and those of us who are trying to foresee just what the consequences of this growing instability will be are few in number.

V

The Powerless Electricians

When executives in industries making a commercial product invest large sums over several years on advertising to
increase the product's sales, it is rare for them to find that
this publicity campaign has been too successful and that
their production capacity is now lower than the demand
—an embarrassment that therefore obliges them to make
heartfelt appeals to their customers to limit consumption
voluntarily.

Yet this is exactly what has happened to companies producing electrical power in the United States. Up to 1968
they were trying to increase consumption by inducing the
public to go in for electric heating and air conditioning.
But in the summer of 1969 they were inviting everyone
to reduce consumption, adding the warning that if such
self-imposed restraint proved insufficient, compulsory rationing would be necessary.

Things are made more difficult in this field because the
building of a new generating station for electric power,
or of a high-voltage transmission line some hundreds of

miles long, may take a few years after the decision is made to do the work. For just this reason it has been impossible for American producers to satisfy in time the demand that they themselves have done so much to create. For the same reason, long-range plans for new production and transmission of electricity should have been deemed indispensable, and adequate resources invested in the necessary research and development. But this did not happen. On average, companies producing electrical power in America in recent years have invested a bare 0.2 per cent of their income in research and development. The Bell System, the largest telephone network in the United States, has spent 1.9 per cent of its revenue on research, but—as we shall be noticing in a later chapter—this has made little impact on the serious situation in which such networks find themselves.

When I was a student at the university of Rome, Italy, in 1950, they taught us that the demand for electric power in the advanced nations doubled every ten years; it was a useful rule of thumb at that time. The same formula repeated twenty years later in *Business Week* (July 11, 1970, page 52) struck me as quaint. It was reporting the estimate made by the Federal Power Commission that the demand for electric power in 1990 will be four times what it was then (which corresponds exactly with doubling every ten years). But the same article had an even quainter look when it stated that "some experts are forecasting a doubling of the demand for power every eight years. . . ." It added that demand is increasing by 12 per cent annually (which would mean doubling approximately every six years). *Business Week* is a serious review, documenting its information with fair accuracy and checking it with federal and industrial sources. As early as November 1969 it had begun to publish forecasts of the power crisis expected in the summer of 1970. The fact that its editorial could report estimates so contradictory, without even pointing out the discrepancy or hinting at the existence of a controversy, is a clear indication that basic knowledge in this field is hazy. Another remark in the same article confirms this impression. It singles out a serious shortage of coal as one of the causes of the power crisis, making vivid use of the fact that in 1969 industry burned 7.8 million tons of coal more than were mined in the same year. This coal deficit would sound impressive to anyone who did not know the total annual production of American coal mines; but as the *daily* average of coal mined in the United States is 2 million tons, it is clear that the coal deficit accumulated in one year corresponds to no more than four days' production, i.e., little more than 1 per cent of annual production—which should not be very worrisome.

But this sytem, too, is so large and complex that no one knows exactly how it functions; or, rather, why it is ceasing to function as it should. As for the supply of coal to power stations—apart from factual difficulties in the mining industry and on the railways (shortage of special freight cars) —it seems that one of the main snags is that the available stocks of coal are not rationally allocated: coal is available, but it is in the wrong places. In the summer of 1969 the stockpiles of the Tennessee Valley Authority were abnormally low, and suddenly they had to decide to transfer 200,000 tons of coal by road from their station at Bull Run to their Kingston station, in order to avoid shutting the Kingston station down. Such facts are a concrete example of my earlier statement—a crisis in one system (here, railway transport) may aggravate a crisis in another system (here, the generation of electrical power).

The difficulties of the producers of electric power are enhanced by the difficulties with which manufacturers of heavy electrical equipment have to contend; they are commonly said to be due, in the main, to shortage of specialist personnel, low productivity, absenteeism, and strikes. But before the turbines or the alternators may be ordered from the manufacturers, authorization has to come from a slow-moving bureaucracy; also, legal disputes may at any time stymie progress. In 1969 United States producers had planned to increase installed power by 26,384 megawatts, but the actual increase was 22,470 megawatts, or 15 per cent below the program.

These inadequacies and delays have worsened the situation in the United States, which is coming to resemble the situation in much less advanced countries—the more so because they themselves have meanwhile been improving. For example, in the fifties, electrical engineers in southern Europe would listen spellbound to marvelous reports about American distribution networks, where no mains failure had been known for over twenty years—whereas in their own countries mains voltage charts presented variations so big that they could be mistaken for charts of electric load. Also, mains failures of varying duration were recorded not just every month but sometimes weekly or daily.

In 1967 the United States began to keep records of the more important breakdowns of service. In two years, from

June 1967 to June 1969, the Federal Power Commission considered 179 cases of breakdown to be important enough for individual analysis, and 80 of these were due to mechanical failure or to faulty operation of the system.

Such critical situations as I have described develop gradually, and are contributory prerequisites of graver crises that will come more precipitately. These are our real interest and concern, for they will be an integral part of that ultimate avalanche of a breakdown which will initiate the dark age.

After the blackout of November 9, 1965, in northeastern United States and in Ontario, another occurred in 1967, affecting the states of Pennsylvania, New Jersey, and Maryland for periods of up to ten hours. In the St. Louis area, during a heat wave in the summer of 1966, the demand for power from air-conditioning plants compelled the Union Electric Company to ration its supply to the city for days on end. Parts of New York were again in darkness for about four hours in February 1971.

Most interesting here, from the viewpoint of the systems engineer, are the decisions, plans, and remedies that have been suggested or adopted for avoiding repetitions of such total city blackouts; and it is therefore worth examining in detail the conclusions reached by the Federal Power Commission. Its report, in three volumes, was devoted to the co-ordinated planning and operating of large power-generating systems, with a view to ensuring maximum reliability and to avoiding faults and breakdowns in cascade on a regional or national scale.

Charles Concordia of General Electric, who is perhaps the ablest living expert on problems of stability and reliability in large electrical networks, is the author of "Considerations in Planning for Reliable Electric Service."[6] He says that no revolutionary changes are needed to ensure a satisfactory level of efficiency. In projecting, planning, and operating your system the application of sound principles is all that is necessary. A cynic might observe that the normal application of these sound principles would itself constitute a revolutionary change; but to linger over a definition of terms here would be less instructive than to look carefully at the concrete suggestions put forward by Concordia (he modestly says that they are obvious) and to compare them with the findings of the Federal Power Commission's report.

Concordia rightly emphasizes that the great majority of the interruptions in electric service are caused by the peripheral distribution networks and not by the large generating and transmitting systems. But service interruptions caused by the latter have much more massive consequences in that they can produce vast secondary crises in the separate systems of communications, transport, defense, public health, etc. Their consideration is therefore top priority. If we may regard as acceptable an interruption of the service once every five years because of some defect in the distribution network, it is reasonable to infer that interruptions due to the main generating and transmitting systems will take place ten times less often, i.e., once every fifty years, the interruption lasting on the average about one hour. Concordia argues that three main procedures are necessary for reaching this level of performance:

1. Systems generating and transmitting power must be so designed that, for any foreseeable future load, genera-

tion and transmission *capacity* will always be adequate to prevent some incident or other from precipitating conditions that could give rise to a second one. For example, if an alternator goes out of service, the power that it fed to the network before the fault will now be required from the other generators still in service; and this may contribute to the overloading of other alternators which, in turn, may be switched off by the action of automatic safety circuit breakers. This type of cascading fault can propagate itself in a very short time until the whole power generated in a large network is switched off. Moreover, the human operators do not even realize what is happening and cannot intervene manually to control and improve the situation. In the blackout of November 1965 the entire chain reaction was over in four seconds, from the moment in which a circuit breaker set at a wrong threshold had switched off one of the 230 kV lines that brought the power of the Sir Adam Beck No. 2 station at Niagara Falls to the interconnected network of the northeastern region of the United States.

2. Systems generating and transmitting power must be *operated* within such limits as to guarantee that there will be reserves great enough to prevent cascading breakdowns. Taking for granted the capacity margins that are an intended part of the system, this second principle defines the way in which the system should be used; it balances competing considerations. An increase in the number of interconnecting electric lines or a growth in their capacity is generally a positive good, for it allows the demands of vast areas to be distributed in a more balanced way among a larger number of generating stations; but to increase the

lines of interconnection is also to increase the complexity of the system, and this may make efficient automatic surveillance of it so difficult as to be actually impossible. Security margins ought not to be indiscriminately enlarged, therefore. It is equally necessary to have operational information continuously at hand, making automatic interventions simple and effective.

3. But apart from these safety margins in the design and the operation of the system, a critical situation can always develop either when separate and improbable troubles become actual together, or when trouble comes through human error or carelessness. Emergency plans are necessary, therefore, to ensure that service interruptions so caused shall be on a small scale and of short duration. The best way to prevent the snowballing of crises until they reach huge dimensions is to "shed load" or to switch off predetermined portions of the load—normally as a function of lowered frequency. Some users will suffer, but the integrity of the system as a complex whole will be preserved.

Concordia's suggestions are to be found also in the report of the Federal Power Commission; but this bulky report contains much more, and a study of the relative importance that it attaches to the several issues is instructive. The conclusions and recommendations of the commission are presented in nine chapters, subdivided into thirty-four sections.

The first chapter (three sections) deals with the formation of co-ordinating organizations, the second (eleven sections) with the planning of interconnected systems, the third (nine sections) with their operation, the fourth (three sections) with regulations for their maintenance.

The fifth (one section) shows how desirable it is to have standard unified criteria for the design, construction, operation, and maintenance of systems generating and transmitting electrical power. The sixth (three sections) suggests emergency provisions able to ensure unbroken service for defense systems and others of critical importance. The seventh (two sections) asserts that manufacturers should be responsible for testing whether their products—apparatus, machinery, etc.—are sound and acceptable. The eighth (one section) advocates improvement in the professional training needed to produce good technicians and engineers in greater numbers. The ninth (one section) proposes that technical information be exchanged with foreign countries where similar problems are being studied.

The report is obviously reasonable, but it is distressing to notice that five of the sections suggest the setting up of committees or organizations. These, alas, will be more likely to busy themselves with the writing of further reports than with effective action. Anyone who is familiar with the inanity of most conferences of technical experts, and of their fact-finding visits, cannot but shudder at the prospect.

Six of the sections propose that systems should be increased in size. This gives the uncomfortable impression that problems of rationalization have received less attention than those relating to the indiscriminate increase of reserves and of capacity installations. Less enlightened developments such as these lead to the situations that are unstable and unmanageable.

Finally, eight sections deal with emergency provisions

for minimizing the effects of blackouts—a recognition that, despite the precautions cited, blackouts cannot be avoided. It would be too optimistic, perhaps, to maintain that the attention the report gives to these emergency provisions is excessive, denoting a basic doubt as to whether measures to be taken to ensure an uninterrupted service of electric power will really succeed. For the fact is that preparedness for emergencies has not sufficed hitherto; and this is clearly shown by the great blackout of 1965, when large turbo alternators at power stations were seriously damaged, merely because the pumps for the lubrication of their huge bearings were powered by a hookup to the very network that the alternators fed. Vicious circle. The pumps stopped; the alternators seized up and were out of action for months.

The Federal Power Commission rightly insists on what it should have been able to take for granted, i.e., the vital necessity of providing emergency power supplies for *auxiliary* services at power stations—namely, lubrication, communications, and lighting. The same provision is necessary for airports, telecommunication, military and civil defense, government offices, systems of mass transportation, systems of communication and control for space missions, hospital services, and underground railways.

A critical situation similar to the one in the United States also exists in Japan, where the demand for electric power doubles every five years, and where power-transmission lines, old and inadequate, have a very low efficiency and provide extremely low safety margins.

It is difficult to prophesy whether improvements in the generation and transmission of power, now being studied in many countries, will be successful or not. My own estimate is pessimistic.

Utilities must rely more and more heavily on nuclear power stations—at present because of increasingly stringent requirements to clean up pollution and therefore to refrain from using high-sulphur fuels, in future decades because of the depletion of natural fuels, particularly oil. Any problem affecting the operation of nuclear power stations will become more and more critical and will eventually entail serious limitations to be imposed on power consumption. It is to be expected in the normal course of events that the production of nuclear power will meet more or less serious snags in the future. Already in the summer of 1972 a new type of fault was found in the unpressurized fuel rods of the reactor in a 490-megawatts power station in Ontario, New York. Until the cause of the fault is found, this reactor—as well as others of the same type for a total capacity of over 7,000 megawatts—must operate at about 60 per cent of capacity.

Power systems appear to be caught between two fires: too much power on networks which are too complicated leads to instability; and, insufficient power in the grids may block all other systems and the whole of society.

A last point. Acts of sabotage and the non-co-operation of consumers led by protest groups could constitute a further negative factor here. If the systems had greater stability than they have, it would not be worthwhile even to mention this kind of marginal factor. But within a few years the effect it might have would not be negligible: it might perhaps be the straw that would break the camel's back.

VI

Urban Congestion and Traffic Paralysis

It was a Wednesday in June 1953, and the streets in the center of Rome were thronged with cars of all types. There were coaches filled with tourists and ancient trucks. There were prewar cars and little utility Fiats. There were people cruising around merely to show off their new 1100—its coachwork modernized at last—or their brand-new sedan. Although license plates in Rome at that time had not yet reached the 200,000 mark, the capacity of the streets in the historic center of the city was much exceeded by the volume of traffic trying to circulate there. Traffic controls were still casual and chaotic, and one of the first big street congestions took place.

On the Via Nazionale movement was by hiccups. Via Quattro Fontane was completely blocked. On the Corso cars were bumper to bumper. In the Piazza del Tritone they were at a standstill for over an hour. After their dusty bus had stood at the same spot in the Via Sistina for half an hour, the members of a municipal band on a visit from the country began to play a little marching song; and at once almost all the bottled-up car drivers began to keep time with the music on their horns. The rhythm spread out over a large area and was taken up even by those who were too far off to hear the band. Pedestrians smiled. Drivers used no bad language, nor were they put out at the unexpected loss of time. There was a festive atmosphere—unjustified, but induced by the sense of satisfaction that in Italy, too, we had reached a motorized level such as to allow us these stoppages and traffic jams, about which we had only read hair-raising and complacent accounts in *Reader's Digest*. A traffic jam in the city for a short time was no confounded nuisance, but a sign of distinction, a status symbol.

Today traffic congestion is recognized by everyone as a plague; it wastes time, causes strain, pollutes the air, and spoils the landscape. Yet strangely enough most people attribute to this evil an inescapable and impersonal character, as though it were a force of nature, such as bad weather. But the events that have taken place in the last twenty years were not too difficult to foresee, nor would it have been too difficult to arrange appropriate remedies in advance. This was not done.

In Rome, for instance, as in New York, the decision was made (blindly, as though implicit in the facts) to carry on as usual, even to use city streets more as stands for stationary vehicles than as channels for vehicles in motion. A quick calculation easily determines what it costs to use a city street as a parking lot. As traffic cannot possibly flow freely along a channel that is occupied by parked cars, a trading loss is inevitable. Add this loss to paving and maintenance costs, and the result is that a parking place for a car on city asphalt is today equivalent on the average to immobilizing capital of $100,000. Such an investment is clearly disproportionate to the advantages that it allows. Furthermore, those who get the advantage are not the same people who pay for it.

The list of events that have been allowed to happen—without any conscious and informed decision being taken to protect or to reach an acceptable state of affairs—is a long one. It has been a series of implicit acceptances of growing evils. We have already noticed that the number of cars in circulation doubles in Italy every four years, and in the United States (where the saturation point is nearer) every fifteen years. But while the number of cars was growing gigantically, the planners lived in hope that somehow everything would turn out all right. In the United States no new system for rapid transportation of masses of people in cities was designed or built for more than sixty years. The first—after this long standstill—is BART (Bay Area Rapid Transit System), in San Francisco and the surrounding Bay Area. The BART took sixteen years—from 1951 to 1967—to be designed, and all but one line of the subway system began operating in May 1973. The new fast trains (which travel at speeds up to 80 mph) began to be used only between Fremont and Oakland, in September 1972.

In Rome there has been half a century of talk about building a subway system, but in comparison with other European capitals design and construction have been ridiculously slow. Work on the Metropolitana began in the early forties, it was resumed after being interrupted by the war, and now after thirty years only one minor branch is in operation.

Linking major cities with their airports by means of fast, reliable, and cheap transport is a world problem; yet it is strange that the fairly obvious solution—a railway from airport to city center—has been adopted only in Brussels, where it has been in successful operation for some years.

We have already noticed that in the United States the annual growth rate of the number of cars in circulation is continuously decreasing, and may be tending toward a foreseeable asymptote. This looks favorable, especially in conjunction with the fact that urban and interurban freeways in the United States are highly developed and widely extended. But at this point two comments must be made. The first is that the cost-benefit ratio for a new U.S. freeway appears to be less favorable than the same ratio for an expanded and improved system of mass transportation; it would be hardly feasible, therefore, to decide on an unlimited proliferation of freeways. The second is that freeway systems are very complicated, abounding in parallel alternative lanes, ramps, and interchanges, the proper use of which is very difficult for drivers who are not familiar with them. This is so, despite official efforts to make the road signs unmistakably clear. To proceed correctly on an average journey in the vicinity of a great city it may be necessary to memorize beforehand the position of a dozen interchange points. Even so, a single mistake may double or treble the length of the journey.

In order to help American drivers, the Department of Transportation has conceived a futuristic scheme of devices, known as ERGS (Electronic Route Guidance System). In this system each vehicle has an automatic "transceiver" installed; before starting on any journey, the driver sets by hand on the transceiver the code appropriate to his destination. The transceiver then transmits this destination code, automatically and continuously. When it passes over a loop of sensitive wire buried beneath the surface of the road, the code is detected and transmitted to a central computer which has time (while the vehicle is still passing over the loop) to determine the next steering maneuver to be made. It sends back through the loop an appropriate signal that lights up a directional indicator on the dashboard. In this way the driver is informed whether, at the next point of decision, he will have to keep straight on or turn left or right; and, as he is guided at all such points of decision, he reaches his destination without trouble.

The cost of ERGS is very high. The transceiver to be installed on each vehicle would cost about fifty dollars if it were to be mass-produced. The Department of Transportation has decided to carry out an experiment on a reduced scale, trying out the system for a few hundred intersections and interchanges in a number of official cars. Recently, however, a shortage of funds has caused even this pilot system to be postponed indefinitely. It would not be so bad if only futuristic innovations were postponed through lack of funds; however, money is lacking for most of the normal "handbook" devices or innovations, in any metropolis in any country.

Soon after World War I, traffic congestion in the United States had reached disturbing proportions in most large cities and towns, particularly in the East. At busy intersections waiting times were becoming longer and longer. In order to avoid these losses of time, Harry Haugh, in 1927, invented traffic-control systems actuated by the traffic itself, and he began to install them in Connecticut.

By means of "detectors"—i.e., sensitive elements buried in the surface of the road—these controls automatically count the number of vehicles approaching the intersection on each street, and either prolong, shorten, or annul the green right of way allotted to each traffic stream in proportion to its numerical strength. If there are no vehicles on one of the streets leading to the intersection, no green signal will be given until some vehicles collect there. This frees other traffic streams from useless stoppages such as occur when red and green periods are unvaryingly equal. Such traffic-actuated lights have obvious advantages which have been duly documented in theoretical studies and practical experiments. And yet before World War II such systems were used extensively only in Britain, and particularly in London, though individual installations were isolated and not integrated in larger co-ordinated systems. In continental Europe they appeared sporadically, and not until the early sixties did they begin to be more widely accepted. One might be tempted to explain this slowness in accepting the more modern system as no more than the familiar technological gap between discovery and its application, were it not that in the United States, where they were invented, traffic-actuated control systems are still in a minority of 30 per cent. Thanks to a conservative attachment to old ways and to ill-conceived budget economies, two thirds of all the new systems of traffic lights installed each year in the United States are still operated by the fixed-time apparatus which is now old-fashioned. It is surely stupid to reject such obvious advantages as this simple and sure technique would provide—a reduction of traveling times by as much as 30 per cent, and a very favorable cost-benefit ratio.

Almost all people who live in cities, especially those who have been driving for some time, regard themselves as experts in the problems of vehicular traffic and suggest strange and gratuitous solutions to the problems of congestion. If they happen to hold important positions, they often pronounce these solutions authoritatively and compel their adoption. We have already noticed how the use of city streets for stationary rather than for moving vehicles has been passively accepted almost everywhere. More radical, and equally ill-informed, solutions are proposed and repeated so often that in due course they may well be put into practice and enforced by law. The idea that they have in common is reduction: compulsory rationing of existing services so as to ensure acceptable traffic conditions—acceptable, that is, for the few who would still be in circulation.

A total ban on all individual and private cars in the centers of cities is mentioned most often as the final solution to this problem. On the assumption that, in the face of present reality and the menace of the future, no other scheme of control can be devised, such a ban would drastically reduce the size of the problem; but it would be throwing out the baby with the bath water.

A similar result could be obtained, of course, by banning the manufacture of new cars or subjecting car production to restrictive quotas. No one has seriously proposed these alternative solutions, however; perhaps because they are absurd, or because the supposed or real power of car manufacturers is feared.

Some success has been achieved by making parking illegal in central urban areas during certain crucial hours of the day. This is confirmation that one of the major factors responsible for urban congestion is the presence of too many parked vehicles in the streets. Eliminating them altogether rather than building off-street parking for them is no solution. In Madrid, Paris, London, and many German and Swiss cities the construction of many underground parking garages has succeeded in easing the flow of traffic without denying to the majority of road users the right to get around. In other words, it is not true that new off-street parking facilities make existing problems worse, because their very availability attracts more traffic: the advantages obtained by freeing the streets outweigh the alleged disadvantages caused by an increase in the total number of vehicles.

I offer these considerations incidentally, and only to show that workable solutions, such as are briefly indicated above, do in fact exist. It is more relevant to my argument that urban traffic systems are not at present "optimized"; they have come into existence in a casual way, and their random development continues unchecked; nor is there any visible sign that some more rational pattern of city administration is on the way. In hardly any of the world's great cities does systems engineering have the rights of citizenship; all decisions are made, rather, in the hope that they will cause the least number of disputes and short-term hostilities—a vague hope that is their only justification.

Even the most trivial expressions of the will of legislators show complete ignorance of the numerical terms of our problem. For instance, illegal parking (and even double parking, which is more detrimental to the flow of moving traffic) is subjected to a fine that may range from as little as $1.60 in Italy to as much as $40 in the United States (a sum that includes the cost of removing the illegally parked car). But these fines bear no relationship to the fact that a double-parked car robs transit traffic of one lane and, on average, causes an added loss to the other users of the road of $20 to $50 an hour. This fact is obviously powerless against another fact, namely that to increase the fine to $50 or to $100 would be too unpopular.

We find no less ignorance in the discussions and myths currently publicized about traffic control systems. Journalists swing from the one extreme of claiming euphorically that some new "electronic cop" is going to solve all existing traffic problems for good, to the other extreme of poking fun at the more easily ciriticizable shortcomings of existing systems. Admittedly, theirs is no easy job, since the whole field is as debatable—but not as glamorous—as any really difficult field on the frontiers of science. Laymen tend to make light of the issues in debate, alleging that common sense, or an intelligent look at the handbook on the shelf, will solve them. This is too facile. Common sense can be hardly any help at all, and many important decisions are reached by using rules of thumb. One such rule —widely accepted in the United States—is that the right number of traffic lights in an urban area is the number of people living in that area divided by 1,000. This procedure is reasonable, although it certainly cannot guarantee success, since it says nothing about the way in which the lights are to be equipped and interconnected. Throughout Europe, at any rate, even this simple rule is disregarded and the number of traffic lights is, on average, lower than the accepted U.S. standard. In Italy, in particular, technology is less rationalized: traffic lights work more reliably when traffic is light, but they are less able to ensure efficient and speedy changes when it is heavy.

But strangely enough these serious failures in rationalization do not have the enduringly adverse influence and the depressing results that we might expect them to have. We have all read newspaper articles with headlines such as these: The City Is Exploding, The Tide of Steel Is Freezing Solid in the Streets of Our Cities, Auto Traffic in the City Now Slower Than Horse-drawn Carriages. But the reality is different. On most days of the year, getting across any large city takes almost exactly the same time today as it took ten years ago when the number of cars in circulation was much smaller.

What has happened in recent years is that because of an almost total lack of rational management and acceptable alternatives, road users have been left to their own devices: a self-imposed discipline has been their only possible reaction. Growing numbers of people have refused to accept delays beyond a certain limit in order to get about as usual, and have voluntarily begun to use the car only when on vacation. To shorten the time that they spend in traveling on weekdays, they have gone to live closer to where they work; they have staggered their usual engagements, used public transport, done more walking; a few have brought the bicycle down from the attic or the scooter up from the cellar. The result is that the volume of traffic actually flowing through the center of a city during weekdays is not very different from what it was five or ten years ago. Exceptional circumstances apart, it is still possible to drive six or seven miles across the center of New York, Boston, Rome, or Paris in little more than half an hour. What *is* worrisome, of course, is that the exception steadily becomes the rule. Ten years ago it would happen about once every six months that one took twice as much time as on other days to get from point A to point B in a large city. Five years ago the same exceptional slow-up happened once a month; today it is every two weeks. Indeed, every six months one now needs three or four hours to drive three or four miles.

Whenever some 10,000 or 100,000 motorists are delayed for more than an hour or so on their customary routes, the mounting vexation is enormous; and on the days following such a city-wide traffic jam there is a marked drop in the number of cars in circulation—some 70 or 60 per cent of what is usual. But in less than a week, as the memory of the jam recedes, the volume of traffic swells again and travel times lengthen. In other words, on an almost horizontal plane representing travel time, an occasional peak of increasing height occurs, with increasing frequency. Each peak is followed by a steep downward slope into a trough (the shorter travel time when vexed drivers are absent from the scene), after which there is a gradual rise to the level plane again.

This pattern of things is easily explained. Motorists'

self-imposed restrictions on their use of their cars means an ever increasing number of cars that *could* begin to circulate at any moment but that are actually kept at home for most of the time. No law or other authority decides whether this enormous reservoir of rarely used vehicles shall flow or remain still. The huge number of these unmoving movers, and their owners' arbitrary decisions about them, constitute an indeterminate or chance phenomenon. As the dimensions of this potential volume of traffic grow, there is the not-to-be-discounted possibility that on some odd day too many cars will suddenly appear on the streets and a king-size traffic jam will be the result. The increasing frequency and gravity of traffic jams is sufficient proof of this.

Recent history and personal experience have a notable effect on phenomena of this kind. Twenty years ago in the United States, when the total number of cars on the roads had not reached 50 million, dreadful traffic jams lasting a couple of days could occur, with the police taking bottles of milk by helicopter to the children of stranded families. In the United States today there are more than 100 million cars, but congestion on the roads is now less distressing—not so much because there are more freeways but because motorists have learned to avoid such risks.

In Europe, where a big jam has rarely lasted for a whole day, the unit of time for measuring the duration of serious traffic congestion is still the hour, rather than the day or the week. But in both Europe and the United States there is a growing assumption that congestion on street and freeway does not greatly matter: it is a serious inconvenience rather than a frightening menace. This quite unjustifiable confidence, together with the uninterrupted addition of new cars to those already in circulation, will be among the causes of the monstrous traffic jams of the future. Not necessarily a distant future. Traffic jams may occur suddenly and for no particular reason, except the coincidence of chance happenings such as a rainy day or a strike of workers in public transport, which will be additional inducements for crowding the roads with cars. And then every mile of every traffic lane in the city will contain three hundred cars, the speed of which will be exactly zero. It will be impossible to disentangle the mix-up in squares and at intersections, and many drivers will abandon their useless vehicles, locking the doors to express their irritation. Such a traffic block will last many days; perhaps weeks. The mess will be so huge that it will be impossible to clear it; rare and improvised efforts may be made by volunteers to nibble at its margins; the return to normality will be slow.

So grievous a crisis—which could quickly have the dimensions of a catastrophe—could happen now, at any moment; its secondary consequences would include the stoppage of much more than private cars. Neither fire engines, doctors, nor police would have free passage and access; and—much more serious—the transport and distribution of food to the large masses of people involved would be virtually impossible. The exhaust fumes of hundreds of thousands of immobilized cars would have ample distribution during the few hours in which there would still be hope of reaching home on wheels.

The events that I have described could well be the first term of a terrible chain reaction leading to worse breakdowns, to the death of megalopolis and to a new dark age.

The phenomena of congestion—usual and familiar, and less deadly than those just described—may be studied and anticipated mathematically. The same mathematical relationships apply, for instance, to the congestion of conversations and service demands on telephone lines as to traffic congestion on the streets. I have tackled the latter first because it is much more dangerous than the former. If you dial a number and fail to get through to the party you want, you can easily get out of the system simply by hanging up. But if you are stuck in a traffic jam within the ton of steel that is your car, you can, at most, abandon the car and go away on foot. There is no simple way whereby you can make the vehicle disappear from the congested system. Again, if two conversations happen to be transmitted simultaneously on the same line, the cross-talk can be embarrassing; but if two cars try to occupy the same position in space simultaneously, they may be permanently damaged and their occupants injured or killed.

If we consider air traffic, things are even worse. In fact, it is impossible not only to remove airplanes from a congested air space by simple and instantaneous means, but also to keep them indefinitely in the congested situation. If the aircraft cannot be landed before its fuel supply is exhausted, it will crash. That is an outcome so obviously to be avoided that up to now there are no known cases in which an airplane has crashed because it has exhausted its fuel and crowded air corridors have delayed its landing. Air traffic controllers always maintain ample safety margins, forbidding take-off to planes that might later crowd the air space over the port of arrival. Indeed, it has actually happened that in order to maintain strict conditions of safety, airplanes have been kept waiting on the runway with their jet engines running so long that they have at length exhausted all their fuel and been forced to go back and refuel, before getting in line again for green-light clearance.

Air traffic congestion takes place both in the air and on the ground. This means, more precisely, in the air corridors predetermined for the different flight paths; on take-off and landing strips; on interconnecting and marshaling runways; and on terminal parking spaces for planes.

The congestion of airplanes in flight means, first of all, that air traffic control systems operate very near the limit of their performance. Flight conditions are therefore becoming less and less safe, as is proven by the increasing number of near misses or close shaves (collisions in flight only just avoided). The congestion of air space also involves very considerable delays in landings, because it is necessary to separate in *time* the aircraft that control systems barely succeed in separating in space.

Congestion on the ground at airports adds further delays to those already experienced before landing. This is due to the waiting times on the runways. The fact is that each airplane cannot extricate itself at all quickly from the tangled web of the slip streams caused by planes that are taxiing between airstrips and parking places. The problem is so serious that the Port of New York Authority recently earmarked $400,000 for the design of the Surface Traffic Control System (STRACS) developed by the Transportation Systems Center of LFE Corporation. This system will determine, by means of detectors, the presence and the passage of airplanes taxiing on the ground at airports; it will be able to follow them and to control their paths, stopping them short, by means of light signals, at points where they would be in conflict with the trajectory of other aircraft on the ground, of service vehicles, or of emergency vehicles. STRACS will control right-of-way priorities and so make the time spent in transit as short as possible. In other words, traffic lights are needed for airplanes, too, as they taxi on the runway.

Even more essential, of course, is the control of aircraft in flight. Though tridimensional radar will not be used for commercial air traffic for some time to come, the Automated Radar Terminal System (ARTS) will be used in the not too distant future on an adequate scale. ARTS will enable air traffic controllers to identify the luminous spots made by aircraft on the radar screen, since these spots will be automatically marked with the alphanumeric indication of the flight number. At the same time the height of each aircraft will be explicitly indicated on the radar screen in luminous figures.

But, as usual, automatic control systems will not be able to compensate indefinitely for the imbalance between the continuous growth of air traffic and the dimensions of aircraft on the one hand, and the scarcity of airports and of airport facilities on the other. It has been estimated that between 1970 and 1980 it will be necessary to build more than eight hundred new airports—an investment of about one billion dollars. It would also be necessary to enlarge existing airports. But it is not difficult to foresee that both new constructions and improvements to existing structures will proceed slowly, and will arrive too late.

J. H. Shaffer, administrator of the Federal Aviation Agency, has stated bluntly that between 1970 and 1980 chaos will be unavoidable at airports and in air transportation systems because there will be a delay of something like ten years before the existing situation can be modified to an appreciable extent. Coming from an administrator, this medium- or long-term forecast may sound pessimistic; but most of the relevant facts show convincingly that it is, if anything, too optimistic.

Inherent in all air transport is a further difficulty which is getting worse: airplanes are becoming more and more noisy. Jet planes make more noise than propeller planes; the supersonic transport is even more noisy than jet planes of the present day. The consequence is that people who live in areas where new airports are projected, or where the enlargement of existing airports is being considered, will oppose these new constructions in order to protect the quiet of their homes; and they will succeed at least in delaying, if not in preventing, a start on the work of construction.

Air transport discloses a familiar pattern. In the initial period of their availability, the short-term advantages of new technical inventions and of new machines—airplanes —have been exploitable without presenting very serious problems. But as these new things are used by people whose numbers are growing exponentially, the medium- and long-term difficulties about congestion are felt in all their weight. We get a glimpse of just how large and serious the "systemistic" problem of air transportation is when we realize that the maximum number of airplanes simultaneously in flight over the United States is at present about fourteen thousand, and that most of them are not controlled from the ground and do not follow instrumental flight rules, but are flown by pilots whose only method is visual control.

It is interesting to examine the forecasts made by William W. Seifert, director of the Transport Project at the Massachusetts Institute of Technology, in a paper that he presented in May 1968 at a seminar of the Institute of Electrical and Electronics Engineers. Seifert assumes that in 1993 the population of the United States will be 300 million (as compared with the present figure of 200 million) and that the number of cars will have grown from the present level of 100 million to 200 million. In these conditions Seifert anticipates that the problem of urban traffic will be solved only in the relatively few cities of entirely new construction, by means of a separation on different levels of pedestrian traffic, car traffic, and parking. In existing cities, despite the construction of many rapid transit systems on rails, traffic congestion will become an abiding fact of life with average speeds of less than eight miles per hour, and with very frequent total traffic blocks of many hours' duration. The only big innovation for road traffic will be automated highways on which individual vehicles will no longer be steered manually but will be automatically controlled by means of electronic apparatus installed in the vehicles, and receiving appropriate signals from a cable buried along the highway's length. According to Seifert, airlines will transport 700 million passengers a year (as compared with the 130 million of 1968). The numerous small airports of new construction will be reserved for vertical-take-off-and-landing

aircraft (VTOL) and for short-take-off-and-landing aircraft (STOL). Conventional railways will have been
completely abandoned and replaced by small wagons automatically controlled, which will proceed on an air cushion
rather than on wheels and be moved by linear induction
electric motors.

Seifert's anticipations seem to me to lack elementary
common sense and to be completely unrealistic. It is unthinkable that road traffic will be slowly degraded until it
assumes characteristics that no one would in fact accept.
On the contrary, phenomena of degeneration will be sudden and brutal, and they will lead to a radical change in
the situation. Any deterioration of efficiency in a transportation system below a given level—however low we
assume this level to be—will necessarily mean that the
system will be abandoned by masses of people until a
fairly small number are left using it, for whom it still has
its advantages. Those who have abandoned the system
(assuming that they are still alive) will have to accept a
drastic diminution in their mobility and probably a simultaneous, marked drop in their standard of living.

Seifert is an authoritative voice from one of the world's
most advanced and competent centers of research pro-
nouncing on two urgent problems. The very fact that he
proposes a complicated solution for the relatively simpler
problem (freeway traffic control), but contends that there
is no solution to the problems of urban traffic, shows that
in the foreseeable future really good solutions are very
unlikely.

Seifert's futuristic visions are just as unsatisfactory,
since they concentrate on separate technical innovations

such as very fast trains supported on air cushions, or VTOL and STOL aircraft, but not on integrated and world-wide solutions. Like too many others, Seifert pronounces the correct formulas:

> The Federal Government has to begin looking at the entire problem of transportation as a system, and to begin moving toward the development of an interrelated group of transport systems, each handling that part of the total for which it is best suited, and each providing convenient interfacing with other modes.

But he does not succeed in filling these formulas with adequate plans. As long as things proceed in this way—and there is no sign that they are about to change—transportation systems will continue to become more unstable, and the danger presented by their paralysis will become more serious and more deadly.

VII

Crisis in Communications

One of the criticisms that planners of collectivist leanings
make against capitalism is that free, or allegedly free, competition is harmful: it wastes vast wealth on advertising
and is forever multiplying its efforts to produce goods that
differ from one another in minor details only—a specious
variety which gives the public no real additional advantage. The sole purpose of the capitalist system is to make
the profits of huge industrial and commercial complexes
as large as possible. The contention, then, is that a much
more efficient use of resources and better quality in goods
and services could be obtained if there were no competition, but a central authority that would define the essential details of what was to be manufactured, when and by
whom; in short, a publicly controlled monopoly.

If there has ever been an industrial group enjoying almost all the imaginable advantages of a monopoly situation—and which has also been subjected to the fairly
efficient control of a public power such as the Federal
Communications Commission—that group is certainly the

American Telephone & Telegraph Company. For nearly a hundred years it has had the monopoly of the manufacturing of telephones and of the construction and operation of telephone networks in the United States. We might well expect that the successes of this gigantic company would therefore be quite extraordinary—at least from the point of view of its earnings, if not from that of the quality of the service it supplies. And it has undoubtedly become a giant, thanks to its continuous profitability. Under the ownership of A.T. & T., the Bell System incorporates the Long Lines Division, the Bell Telephone Laboratories (which carry out basic research), Western Electric (which manufactures equipment), and twenty-four companies responsible for regional operations. The Bell System may also boast of the scientific innovations produced within the company—an impressive record that includes the transistor, invented in 1948, and information theory developed by Claude Shannon when he was working for the Bell Laboratories.

In spite of all these advantages, Ma Bell is now in serious trouble. In fact, the deterioration of telephone systems in the United States has been all the more startling in that, until very few years ago, the Bell System was considered the most modern and efficient in the world. It is significant that the deterioration started during the second half of 1968, in areas where urban concentration is very dense, and particularly in the city of New York where the situation was truly grim by 1969. Delays of service, the sheer impossibility of calling many parties, the number of faults that went unrepaired for days or weeks on end, had produced such a situation that a large advertising firm,

Benton and Bowles, Inc., bought a whole page in the New York *Times* in order to publish the names of its eight hundred employees with this short comment: "Perhaps you don't believe that all these people are still working for us because you cannot speak with them over the telephone; but they are all still here. Come and see us and you will meet them."

Ironically the head office of A.T. & T. was virtually unreachable by telephone for many months because it was connected to the automatic switchboard Plaza 8, one of the most congested. The New York Telephone Company of A.T. & T. group was sued for damages totaling some $330 million by a group of citizens of the Bedford-Stuyvesant district who complained of the deterioration of service during the previous three years.

The plight of American telephones typifies that "breakdown of large systems" which is the main theme of this book. We recognize in it all the remote and immediate causes of deterioration and the standard features of their effects.

With subscribers in excess of 100 million the U.S. telephone system is very large; it has grown very rapidly, doubling in less than twenty years, and it is highly concentrated. New York City alone has 11 million subscribers and accounts for more than 10 per cent of the 350 million phone calls made every day in the United States.

The main cause of the crisis may be ascribed to serious errors in forecasting. In 1967 the New York Telephone Company foresaw a leveling off in the increase of the gross national product and deduced that the demand for telephone service would have grown in 1968 by no more than

4 per cent; the company therefore reduced its budget for new constructions by $24 million. But in 1968 and 1969 several facts caused the demand for telephone service to increase suddenly and on a massive scale. There was increased activity on the Wall Street stock exchange, an increase in the transmission of digital data on telephone lines between processing centers for electronic data, and the welfare agencies decided to reimburse their clients for their telephone bills. In addition, it seems that people began to use the telephone more, simply because they stayed at home longer, to avoid traffic jams and crime in the streets; and when they did go out, they left the telephone off the hook so that thieves might believe someone was at home if they made a check call before trying to break in. Thanks to the cumulative effect of facts such as these, the operation of the old-fashioned switchboards that are still widely in use was seriously impeded.

At first, that sudden increase in the demand-curve was regarded as a temporary aberration. But the curve did not level off as expected; it went up and it stayed up.

Now that there is a crisis, the size of which is apparent even to the least attentive observer, the New York Telephone Company has decided to increase its annual investment in apparatus and facilities to the level of a billion dollars; the corresponding figure budgeted by A.T. & T. for the whole of the United States is $7.5 billion. But delays in delivery on the part of manufacturers, and delays caused by technical interruptions, will prevent the effects of any remedial action from being felt before two or three years have elapsed.

The second cause of the crisis is financial. A long-term

forecast has indicated that before 1979 A.T. & T.'s budget will have to reach $150 billion merely to keep up existing services, to extend them in the near future to video-telephones, and to increase them in accordance with demand. The capital needed for such an outlay is enormous. A.T. & T. are hopeful rather than confident that they will secure it by offering private investors 200 million new shares and a comparable issue of debentures. They also intend to increase tariffs which, at present, should produce an increase of some $2 billion in annual revenue. A tariff increase is no routine matter, however. It has to be approved by the Federal Communications Commission, which will certainly be opposed to some of A.T. & T.'s requests; and although this restrictive action of the commission may mean short-term advantages for telephone users, it will probably oblige them to put up with the long-term disadvantages of permanently impaired service. We must add that the $150 billion necessary during the next ten years will not be enough to modernize the Bell System completely, even though the outlay represents 15 per cent of the gross national product of the United States at the level of 1971. In fact, it has been foreseen that the passage from traditional telephone switchboard to completely electronic switchboard will not be completed before the year 2010.

The mistaken decisions of American telephone companies have been caused, in part, by an excessive trust in technical innovations such as the entirely electronic switchboards just mentioned. They operate at a much higher speed than that of electromechanical switchboards. In the future, the use of the new switchboard will offer marked advantages, but at the moment it is causing serious trouble. This should not be cause for scandal, of course. When any new and complex product is first used, snags are only to be expected; and this is particularly true when some large innovation is made in a vital part of an existing system. Engineers are as familiar with teething troubles as anyone else.

The difficulties all add up, and the management of A.T. & T. has not been able to adopt timely remedial action. Their official answer to criticisms made to them from many quarters was that nobody could have foreseen such a sudden increase in the demand for telephone service. All the same, the president of the New York Telephone Company was replaced. The present president, William M. Ellinghaus, will have to improve the performance not only of the group managers, but also of employees at the level of switchboard operators and maintenance crews. The competence of the latter has deteriorated sadly. In 1969, 40 per cent of personnel of this type had had less than one year's experience in their jobs. (It is only fair to add, however, that at the present time it would require real artists to install and maintain telephone cables in Manhattan, where there is just no space left beneath the streets.)

The problems of telephone networks not only justify pessimistic conclusions; they will become more critical still because of the fast-growing diffusion of lines for transmitting digital data to and from electronic computers at great distances from one another.

It is well known that in the United States long-distance calls by means of the WATS system (Wide Area Telephone Service) suffer longer delays between 5:30 P.M. and 7:00 P.M. on weekdays than at other times. This is so because between those hours the branches of banks and the peripheral offices of commercial companies transmit the accounting data of the day to central computers, some of which may be hundreds of miles away. This type of communication is used on an increasing scale. The president of A.T. & T., Frederick R. Kappel, stated in 1961 and again in 1964 that within fifteen years the volume of communications between computers by data transmission would become far larger than communications by the human voice. What Kappel meant is not quite clear because he did not specify whether he was referring to the number of calls or to the quantity of information transmitted. A controversy on this point is still going on between A.T. & T. spokesmen and, among others, Roger W. Hough, of Stanford Research Institute. Hough contends that for the next twenty years communications by voice will keep telephone networks busy for periods of time that will be as long again as those of all other types of communication put together. This statement sounds reasonable, and yet the mere list of all the types of information that can now be transmitted on telephone lines is so long as to suggest that the sum of them will greatly add to the load of telephone systems, worsening their congestion and their instability. One has only to reflect on what, in fact, it is possible to send by telephone: video-telephone pictures, television programs, facsimile transmissions of newspapers, the printing of books at a distance, signals allowing data stored in electronic memory banks and specialized information centers to be automatically retrieved, data for the automatic reservation of seats on travel systems, data relating to stock exchange transactions, etc.

The crisis in telephone systems will get worse as time goes on, but we cannot really expect that it will directly cause destruction and death, except in exceptional circumstances. For example, failure to get through on the phone may cause the deaths of a few people: fire equipment or doctor does not arrive in time. The damage caused by the flood of 1966 in Florence would have been much less if the telephone link between the watch stations upstream and the city authorities had been better and quicker. In general, however, the crisis in telephone and telegraph systems will worsen the critical situation in other systems that will be called on to function in place of the unusable wire and cable services. (A typical case is that of A who is unable to get through to B by phone, and therefore tries to reach B in person by taking out the car, only to worsen the traffic jam that has already begun.) It will also prevent the flow of information about any other emergency, putting additional obstacles in the path of maintenance and rescue teams. It is noteworthy, too, that as soon as some abnormal fact is "news," the almost automatic reaction of large numbers of people is to get on the phone to talk about it. When Franklin D. Roosevelt died on April 12, 1945, an enormous number of people tried to call someone on the telephone about the news. As a result the entire telephone network of the United States (which then connected fewer than 30 million subscribers) was blocked for several hours.

As in other cases, I have first considered the situation

in the United States because concentrations are higher in the United States than elsewhere, and the corresponding crises ripen earlier than in other countries. But the situation is not very different in, say, France. To get a new telephone installed in the Paris area takes about a year. The engineers of a large electronic construction company that has its research center in Monthlery, about sixteen miles south of Paris, have to wait three or four hours every morning before they can speak with the headquarters of the company in the Boulevard Bessières in the 17th arrondissement. The Italian situation, deplorable until a few years ago, has been improved with the extension of direct dialing to connect all the 9 million subscribers in the country; but it is still far from satisfactory. European systems are being interconnected in a single network, the dimensions of which are continuously becoming larger; and this will increase the probability of congestion due also to growing concentrations of people in capitals and other large cities.

A system of communications that has repeatedly hit the headlines in recent times is the national and international postal service. It is rarely efficient, and its inadequacies are publicized as mainly due to strikes.

Mail and telephone are two very closely connected systems, each of which can partially replace the other. During the long postal strikes of 1969 in Italy and of 1971 in England it became a common habit not only to send information by telephone that previously went by letter, but also to use the same technique for reaching formal commercial agreements. The texts of contracts that the mail service might be delivering weeks or months later (or perhaps never) were meanwhile dictated over the phone.

The postal systems of the United States and of Italy are strikingly similar, notwithstanding the great difference between their respective dimensions. More than 80 billion items a year are handled by the U.S. mail; fewer than 6 billion items are handled by the Italian—a difference in magnitude, incidentally, that is indicated by other statistics: U.S. GNP in 1970 was about $1,000 billion; Italy's GNP in the same year about $80 billion; the annual number of cars produced in the United States about 12 million; the corresponding number for Italy, 1.3 million. Note, however, that the U.S. population is only four times larger than the Italian population.

Among the deficiencies common to the Italian and the U.S. postal systems are:

* inefficiency, and delays in deliveries
* old-fashioned organization
* low productivity and low salaries of personnel
* high frequency of strikes
* very high operational deficit ($1.2 billion at the end of 1970 in the United States)
* very low success in the use of ZIP codes.

There are idiosyncrasies in each country, of course. In Italy, for example, there are frequent and absurd delays (up to a week) in the delivery of night letter cables; and an equally absurd delay is caused by the American obsession with the discovery and indictment of anyone sending obscene literature by mail. But apart from these idiosyncrasies, the main difference between the two countries is that in America the government mail system is not a monopoly—private competitors are allowed, whereas in Italy this is illegal, except for certain small-scale urban delivery services. Another difference is that Italian administrators and politicians are more optimistic than their American counterparts; they speak very highly—at least in public—of the efficiency and the bright future of their system or ministry, though each is sadly different in reality. The Americans are more candid in their criticism and more realistic in their evaluations. It is instructive to examine some statements and proposals.

The Postmaster General of the Johnson Administration, Lawrence F. O'Brien, admitted that his department was involved in "a race with catastrophe," and on April 3, 1968, he proposed that the U.S. Post Office should be transformed into a nonprofit government agency. This type of reform (finally adopted by the second Nixon Administration) was intended to give a certain independence to the Post Office administration, permitting the elimination of the deficit, improving the service and the working conditions of the employees, and taking away from the political parties the right to control promotions and to hand out jobs. Formerly the unions of Post Office workers were not even in a position to negotiate directly, because any improvement in wages could be decided only by Congress. The Postmaster General in the Nixon Administration, Winton M. Blount, had defined the Post Office Department as "a high-cost labor-intensive anachronism"; the necessity of reform is inescapable. As usual, reform of the system itself should take precedence over purely technical improvements, however desirable: the problems of a large system cannot be solved simply by using new automatic machines. It appears, however, that in the United States excessive hopes are being placed on the advantages to be obtained by the increased use of automatic sorters (already in partial use with appreciable success for more than ten years) and by the installation of automatic optical scanners. Semiautomatic sorting machines—on each of which up to twelve operators may work simultaneously —automatically distribute the items of mail among 277 outputs, provided that the operator has indicated on a keyboard the correct code of the output required for each item. (He deduces this from the address, using a set of equivalents that he has had to memorize.) The errors made by these machines, each of which can classify up to 36,000 letters an hour, amount to just over 5 per cent. Automatic optical scanners work much better if addresses have been typed with special characters. A research project (which will probably be useless) is at present aiming at the design of an automatic machine that will be able to read handwritten addresses.

I do not want to contend that automatic or semi-automatic machines are useless. On the contrary, the postal situation would be much healthier if these machines were used on a larger scale. I do contend, however, that while it is possible to improve the performance of postal systems even without using new machines, it is certainly conceivable that new machines might be employed and yet the system's performance continue to deteriorate because its structure had not been modified.

In this context it is worth referring to the Swedish postal system, which is considered to be the most efficient in the world, although it has to ensure deliveries and collections scattered over great distances in the far North. Swedish mails earn a profit of about 1.5 per cent on their modest yearly turnover of $280 million, and they ensure delivery within twenty-four hours of 90 per cent of their letters, parcels, etc. The stamp for a normal letter costs ten cents.

Such evidence may be considered marginal; but it may perhaps suggest that from other viewpoints, too, large systems do better in Sweden than in other countries. Concentrations of population are limited there (throughout Scandinavia there is no city with more than a million inhabitants); systems are not too large and not congested; the levels of technical competence are very high. These facts may preserve Sweden's systems from deterioration and the country itself from an imminent dark age.

An encouraging sign from Sweden does not justify optimism about the rest of Europe. Similarly we ought not to cherish high hopes for the future of the United States because of good news from Nebraska. (In terms of population Nebraska, with its 1.5 million inhabitants, is the thirty-fifth state in the United States.) But in Nebraska local authorities and the Department of Transportation have launched "Project 20/20," which is intended to create an integrated system of all emergency communications in the region. D. G. Penterman, the author of the scheme, has set up centers for all calls addressed to the organizations responsible for each type of emergency. Nebraska has thus been able to reduce its number of continuously manned centers because the same centers will deal in turn with medical care, traffic incidents, crime, civil commotion, fires, and natural disasters. At the same time all the systems of communication in the state have a unified design to ensure that each network, when it is not in actual use, may be available for purposes different from its statutory purpose. Even the emergency channels for communicating the needs of military and civil defense are also used for day-to-day services of public interest. The result has been a striking increase in efficiency, though this is not easily measurable; also a saving of money and resources so considerable that it pays for the whole scheme as well as for the state's educational program on TV.

The example set by Nebraska has not been followed by other states in the Union or by other American organizations. It is the familiar story of "where there's a will there's a way": in this case a man and a group of enlightened people, informed and willing to act to make things work. The places are rare where such things happen.

VIII

Electronic Computers: Some Unjustified Hopes and Fears

"Digital computers are electronic brains."

"Digital computers operate faster than human brains and make fewer mistakes in calculation."

"Any large systemistic problem can be defined by a mathematical model."

"It is certainly advantageous to use digital electronic computers to solve any problem of data processing, or to control any great system."

"Once the responsibility for operating all large systems has been delegated to electronic computers, there is a risk that these machines will replace man completely and will turn him into a slave."

Unfortunately these statements constitute the only justification for many decisions that attempt to solve problems involving millions of people. Moreover, it is just this type of decision that is considered particularly modern and enlightened; whereas some of the five statements quoted are devoid of any meaning, and others can be considered true only in special contexts and in the light of accurate predeterminations.

Almost everyone likes to obtain the maximum result with a minimum of effort, and it is no great wonder that many men having to make important decisions hope to avoid hard work and to shirk important decisions by acquiring a large electronic computer. The ostensible reason for this decision is that the automatic processing of data will ensure that the whole system will be operating at its best; the processing will be flexible, too, and will therefore guarantee that the type of strategy chosen may be instantly brought up to date when necessary, and its programs deftly modernized. This will allow the incorporation of any new ideas and solutions that may have cropped up in the meantime.

But it should be obvious that in lotteries of this kind one never wins. If the single-thread design, the structure and the logic of the system, has not already been properly defined, and if the problems that produce the eventual congestion of the system have not been solved, no appreciable advantage will be obtained merely by using a computer. In fact, whenever a computer is installed without the necessary systemistic analysis having first been carried out, it often happens that the computer programs are made to incorporate strategies and systemistic structures of the simplest possible kind, so that there may be no risk of failure on a big scale. There are systems in

existence in which a certain number of processes are controlled by means of an electronic digital computer, and
are accordingly rated as very modern and efficient, whereas
in actual fact they supply a very modest and uninteresting
performance.

The very concept of flexibility deserves a brief discussion at this point, since for the past twenty years the literature of most computer manufacturers has been boasting
about this asset that their machines are alleged to have.
When we say that an electronic digital computer is a very
flexible machine, we really mean that it is not a machine
built for a special purpose, but that it can be used to solve
mathematical and logical problems of many different
kinds, provided of course that someone has previously
prepared the programs necessary to supply the required
solutions. This task—writing programs, or producing
entire program libraries and programming systems to enable a computer to solve certain problems—is often under-
estimated. Moreover, in many cases it costs much more
than the processing and the auxiliary equipment installed
in the center, since highly specialized manpower and the
time required by a computer for program testing have to
be paid for.

The two terms that have been coined for concise and
convenient reference to all this are "software" and "hardware." Software defines the *performance* of computers,
which is made possible by the equipment that carries out
the appropriate operations; but this performance derives,
of course, from the operational possibilities offered by the
libraries of programs, the auxiliary programs, and the availability of symbolic programming languages. Hardware, on

the other hand, uses its literal meaning to indicate the actual machines or physically existing pieces of equipment of which the data processing computer is made up.

It is clear, then, that when the manufacturer of computers claims flexibility for his machines, he is underlining an indisputable truth. With equal plausibility the truck manufacturer may claim flexibility for his trucks because they can carry canned beef, books, electrolytic condensers, or pumpkins. With the truck, you merely load and drive off, whereas with the computer, you must first prepare the necessary software—the prior and effective programming of your problems—before the computer can handle them. In short, the flexibility of computers is no guarantee that any task assignable to the software can actually be carried out, nor that it can be carried out economically.

The programs, the software, and the general way in which a computer is used cannot be better or more efficient than the programming personnel that has produced them. During the last twenty years the demand for programmers, software experts, and analysts has grown very fast, and it has been necessary to train new recruits too quickly. Faulty training of programmers and the meager experience of many instructors have certainly contributed to many large-scale failures of data processing even in very big industrial organizations. Instead of making the processed data available more quickly and more accurately, computers have meant long delays and frequent errors; instead of supplying at least an equivalent level of service at lower cost, they have pushed costs up. In recent years, therefore, many large industrial and commercial concerns have decided to minimize the risks they run by going in for automatic data processing, and have put the whole job, by contract, into the hands of companies who specialize in this field. I report these facts simply to emphasize that the application of electronic processing systems is a serious business. Not all problems can be solved by buying or renting a computer and hiring a few engineers and mathematicians.

In one sense it is a pity that the successes of research laboratories and of the electronic industry have had so much publicity. This induces the more up-to-date and progressive scientists in almost every field to conceive and plan solutions to their problems simply in terms of hardware and software, rather than in systemistic terms.

For example, when a bank mechanizes the huge mass of work involved in the accounting operations of its several offices, the fact that gets all the limelight is that the arithmetical and operational part of the work is done by a computer; the very important work of procedural analysis that has to be carried out before the mechanization, and that often entails deep modifications in the whole operation, is thrown into obscurity. The analysis of procedures is necessary in order to establish that these procedures can indeed be mechanized, and to make them amenable to the process if they are not so already. When this analysis is done well, it often brings advantages that are at least comparable to, if not greater than, those obtainable by using electronic equipment for data processing: if the analysis is superficial, the entire system will work less well after mechanization than before.

The proper approach to a system consists in the attempt to have it working throughout at its very best, singling

out the data to be processed, avoiding duplications, eliminating any procedure that yields superfluous data, and—
if necessary—defining anew the essential purpose of the
work to be done.

It is well known that apart from their use in the fields
of pure and applied science, electronic computers have
scored their most spectacular successes when applied to
the data processing and accounting already mentioned.
The distinctive fact here is the enormous amount of data
to be processed. Its very hugeness has often been decisive;
it has seemed to make the use of a computer imperative
whenever we are confronted by data in vast amounts,
whereas little consideration has been given to an obvious
alternative, the working out of such modifications in the
system as would prevent its production of data on this
huge scale.

Legal procedure aptly illustrates this—particularly case
law, with its blood bank of data stored up to ensure the
transfusion of healthy legal decisions. Every year the
courts produce opinions and judgments learned in case
law. Every verdict can constitute an important precedent
for the decisions that will be made and the verdicts that
will be pronounced in later trials. This is particularly true
of courts in countries with an Anglo-Saxon tradition,
where precedent—rather than the Codes of continental
Europe—is the main source of law. Their lawyers and
judges have the task of selecting previous judgments that
have some bearing on the case before them. And year by
year they are fated to try to find and identify them from
among an enormous and ever growing number of past
judgments that have no immediate import. The question

now frequently asked, therefore, is whether such judgments might be codified by being distilled or translated into codes which electronic computers can accept and their memories can store. These same computers would be used to retrieve past judgments relevant to a particular present issue, seeking certain key words in their texts that would adequately spell out what the judgment should be. A lot of work has been devoted to research of this kind in the United States, the Soviet Union, England, Belgium, France, Italy, Holland, Luxembourg, Czechoslovakia, West and East Germany. Much less attention—almost none in fact—has been devoted to the reform of law and the juridical system itself, and yet this alone could provide the fundamental solution that would eliminate not only computers, but also the need to hoard a mass of precedent that grows ad infinitum.

Something very similar is taking place in the much wider field of scientific publications. More than 100,000 technical and scientific periodicals are published throughout the world today. Even if a scientist were to consider only those among them that concern his own particular line of research, he could not hope to have time enough to examine all of them to find out whether someone may have already published the results to which his new line of research should lead. Here again the use of electronic computers has been suggested, so that all the technical and scientific publications in the world could be memorized (after being translated into English if they appeared originally in another language). Scientists, research workers, and technicians would then have to investigate this automatic memory, in the attempt to retrieve everything now existing in print that is relevant to the research on which they are currently engaged. Here the problem is indubitably more serious and more critical. Some say that most of a scientist's time is taken up nowadays with bibliographical research, and this is not improbable. It finds support in the fact that there are already 100,000 volumes in existence, containing bibliographies and nothing more (and these are listed in another volume entitled *World Bibliography of Bibliographies*).

But here again it would be more rewarding to analyze the actual process of scientific and technical publication, and of the subsequent use made of it, rather than to accept without question the twofold principle first, that every year thousands of tons of such printed papers should be produced and distributed, and second, that nothing will enable prospective students to find what they need in them, except the sheer power and speed of giant electronic computers.

An obvious authoritarian alternative would be a forcible limitation of the number of articles and papers now printed, and even of the number now produced. Any scientist could supply a long list of publications the printing of which could have been omitted without making much difference to anyone. Nor is this very surprising: true and effective advances in knowledge are not only difficult but rare.

One change that would in itself do much to reduce the colossal number of such scientific publications would be to rid the academic world of the slogan "publish or perish." Many persisting assumptions and procedures for deciding academic merit and promotion need radical revision.

Rightly or wrongly the standing of a university teacher is too often considered a function of the number of pages he has published. This largely explains why younger scholars who aspire to higher rank in the academic hierarchy publish too many papers too often. If the effective criteria in this field were less quantitative, much of their effort could be constructively redirected, and very many papers having little or no enduring value would never see the light of day.

Genuine contributions to science that might be virtually buried and lost when needed could be retrieved satisfactorily if kept in repositories or archives. Here unpublished articles, technical texts, and scientific papers would be stored on microfilm rather than published in magazines or journals. These repositories would publish no more than bibliographies giving titles and short summaries of the papers in their keeping. Occupying little printed space, they could be reproduced in large numbers and distributed among scientists; complete texts would only be available on request.

"Print control" is probably more urgent than birth control. Each presupposes and requires the establishment of a new tradition; but long-term processes yield no short-term solutions, and even electronic computers do not really supply short cuts or immediate answers.

If the advantages that systems managers had hoped to get from the use of electronic computers have not amounted to much, the fault has lain largely with organization. But there is something worse—the fallacies and erroneous concepts that, unfortunately, have free course in the field of electronic computation or "informatics" (as some would like to label this modern science of communication theory and data processing). Computers are used with enthusiasm for many types of scientific research, and for big industry and commerce, thereby attracting large investments of capital. And yet the basis on which such projects rest is vague and unreliable, because of its inherent contradictions and impossibilities. The feature that these fundamental errors have in common is that they assume a more or less definite analogy between the operation of electronic computing systems and the working of the human brain. Indeed, their aim is to produce computer programs in which the computer will replace man, carrying out rational activities and making decisions at a high level. Further, this replacement of man by machine is usually said to be desirable because it is economical. It soon becomes clear, however, that the economies hoped for are not being realized and that the whole project is not really feasible. Its designers now shift their emphasis, therefore, and try to justify the effort already made by contending that it has served a useful scientific purpose: it has proved that very identity of machine with man that was their initial postulate. Or, at least, its work has been an important contribution to the proof of that equation in the future.

The fundamental trouble in this whole matter is probably due to Norbert Wiener. He was a very able mathematician and he enjoyed great prestige. He was therefore listened to and believed when in 1948 he dug up the word "cybernetics" (innocently coined by Ampère 114 years be-

fore in the context of a general classification of sciences)
and claimed to have founded a new science of controlled
communication in animals and machines. And even in the
present day "cybernetics" is not a dirty word either at the
Academy of Sciences of the U.S.S.R. or in the RAND
Corporation; though it should be, as Mortimer Taube
clearly demonstrated as early as 1961 in his brilliant book
Computers and Common Sense.

To understand the issue there is no need to reopen the
old controversy between vitalism and mechanism. No one
disputes that the human brain functions by means of an
aggregate of material within which electric currents flow.
Further, no one denies that there are aggregates of matter
in electronic computers through which electric currents
flow; nor that computers can perform certain operations—
such as the formal (i.e., mechanical) processing of data—far
more rapidly than man can. What must be denied is that
at the present stage of our electronic technique a computer can furnish calculations equivalent to those of a
human brain. It is very probable that the situation is even
more complex than this, if it is true that computers can
only deal with information in accordance with formally
defined processes, whereas the human brain functions in a
way that is essentially informal.

Without trying to solve this very specialized question,
we shall find the history of cybernetics during the last
twenty years instructive enough. In the early fifties it was
not only writers of popularized science but engineers and
mathematicians in charge of advanced research in leading
universities and laboratories who promised that within a

few years computers would be available, programmed in such a way as to be able to:

• produce automatic translations of high quality from one language to another, or at least from English into Russian and vice versa
• demonstrate new and interesting theorems in the fields of mathematics, geometry, and mathematical logic
• play chess at such a level that the world's chess champion would be a machine and not a man
• learn procedures and new concepts, not from what had been formally inserted into the program beforehand, but as fundamental deductions from direct knowledge of the external world

Things have not gone quite like this. The Central Intelligence Agency of the United States is said to produce a computer translation of *Pravda* every day, from Russian into English. Even if this were true, such an activity could hardly be labeled absurd, since even a word-for-word translation (achieved perhaps by listing all the dictionary synonyms of each word in the original text) could give some rough idea of the original meaning. But this would not mean that professionally competent translations from foreign languages could be produced mechanically. That is probably demonstrable on theoretical and conceptual grounds, but they are too complicated to be stated here. Pragmatic proof is clear enough.

Any text written in any language is, in effect, a message sent from one person to another, or to a group. In order to be intelligible it must presuppose a common or shared experience on the basis of which each person has formed in his mind an image or model of the external world. Only by referring to that image or model can anyone receiving the message master its ambiguities and understand its possible neologisms without effort. Until man is able to manufacture electronic computers with a memory able to file or store an image of the external world, they will be unable to give him professionally competent translations, and as I have already hinted, perhaps not even then. Today the memories of computers are still inadequate in this respect, and publishers in particular find it cheaper and more efficient to use human translators.

What about the alleged ability of computers to demonstrate theorems? This is certainly possible, since theorems both in geometry and in logic have been proved by machines. Sad to say, however, the theorems were already well known; our machines have not enabled us to advance a single step along the path of mathematical progress. Perhaps a parallel with spiritualism might be drawn here. I have no very strong reason for not believing that it is possible to communicate with the ghosts of dead people; but until someone succeeds in getting in touch with the ghost of Pierre de Fermat and obtaining from him the proof of his last theorem, I flatly refuse to be impressed.

Similarly it is easy to store in a computer the rules for playing chess; but up till now no computer has been known to play a game at a level higher than that of a good beginner. On December 31, 1971, I won a hundred dollars on a bet that I had made ten years before with Joe Weizenbaum, one of the best-known American specialists in the field of artificial intelligence. I had bet him that on that date the world's chess champion would still be a man and not an electric computer. What Joe's opinion may be to-day I do not know; but I am sure that for several decades to come the world's best chess player will be human; and I am ready to renew the bet.

What of the last promise of cybernetics, that there will be computers able to learn on their own, so to speak— i.e., on the basis of their previous experience? Here opinions differ, since several people maintain that they have already programmed computers in this way; and this, I fear, involves us in a problem in semantics. It is certainly possible to program a computer so that it responds at once to signals coming from the outer world and, with signals of its own, controls the process in hand. It is also possible for the computer to work out statistics on the behavior of the outer world, following procedures that have had to be foreseen beforehand by the programmer and defined by him explicitly and formally. On the basis of these statistics the computer can give appropriate guidance and direction to the equipment—the job it was installed to do. But it is very doubtful whether there is any meaning in the statement often made that a computer can be so programmed that as a result of events (or types of events) it will make its own best possible response, which the programmer has not foreseen and of which he has no knowledge.

Learning machines seem to be used in two main ways. One—in the postal system—is for pattern recognition, which reads handwritten addresses and sends letters by the routes that are proper to their respective destinations.

The other is military: report has it that learning machines have been or might be used for defense.

Here the typical issue is the sudden attack that one superpower could make on another by launching missiles having a nuclear warhead. The power that is attacked has a very short time in which to initiate reprisals; but the decision to launch the nuclear counterattack is so momentous that there must be no risk of a mistake being made. In the United States, at least, this decision may be taken only by the President. A few years ago someone wrote an ostensibly scientific paper entitled "A Program to Simulate the President of the United States"; but neither Johnson nor Nixon delegated their presidential responsibilities to a machine, as a result.

The fact is that this military use of electronic computation is a great unknown: as long as world conflict on a large scale does not happen, no one can know how much success the use of computers would have. It is certain, however, that one of the nations that has made most use of them is the United States (undoubtedly the world's most advanced nation in this field); and if the United States has used them in its conduct of the war in Vietnam, one may conclude that successes in the military field are not more frequent or more probable than those in commercial, industrial, or scientific fields.

It would be wrong to conclude from the foregoing considerations that I regard electronic computers as useless. My contention is that their use cannot of itself solve the problems of management, control, organization, and structure that are now bedeviling large systems and making them uncontrollable and unstable.

One could dispute this, of course, by arguing that the success of the American missions to the moon demonstrates the ability of one of the most advanced nations on our planet not only to bring into being a vast system functioning faultlessly, but also to use electronic computers within that system, perfectly integrated with its other machines and with the people running them, and thereby achieving its purpose and obtaining an almost unimaginable operational precision. The force of this contention is obvious, but there is a threefold objection to it nevertheless. First of all, the spacecraft sent to the moon go and come back one at a time, so that there is no crowding or congestion—at least in the more dangerous and fast-moving phases of the mission. In the second place, the Government of the United States (up to 1969 at any rate) has spent more than $5 billion a year on space programs: this is more than its total expenditure on air transport, water systems, global transport, mail services, regional development, trade controls, and research in the field of atomic energy for military purposes. An investment on this scale deserves to succeed. Third, though this system is splendidly self-authenticating, and has the machines, the men, and the organization necessary for its continuance, the recent cuts in NASA budgets and the striking reduction in American space commitments seem to show that it is lacking in the capacity to ensure its own survival. Is it so very different from all the other systems on the way to breakdown that have been our concern all along?

There remains the fifth of those pronouncements quoted at the opening of this chapter. It expresses alarm at the danger of a total control of individuals by society when it is technically advanced and completely computerized.

There is no denying that financial and fiscal controls can be much more efficient if they are confided to files stored in electronic computers, and it may be noted, in this context, that inasmuch as excessive control over the activities of individuals is regarded as an evil, the inefficiency of systems has its positive value. As usual, then, the gravest risk lies not in the existence of modern mechanisms and automations as such, but in their abuse by individuals in power and by organizations whose aims are intrinsically evil.

It is hardly necessary to remind ourselves that the degradations and annihilations of human beings by industrial techniques operated by the Nazis have not been emulated, even remotely, by any other state power; and yet electronic computers had not been invented when Germany was under the Nazis.

IX

Water and Waste

E. R. Poubelle was thirty-nine when he was decorated with a silver medal for the patriotic part he played during the Prussian siege of Paris in 1870. But his fame rests not on his soldier's record nor on his subsequent popular career as a professor of law. That his name is heard more often than De Gaulle's on Parisian lips is due to the fact that for more than eighty years the dustbins have been called *poubelles*—those large buckets for the reception and collection of refuse which must stand at the street door of every house in Paris, in conformity with an edict of Poubelle's during his prefecture of the Seine (1883–96). The order is still in force, and every evening the inhabitants must deposit garbage and other rubbish in their *poubelles* (which have to conform in size to the standard model approved by the Prefecture). The next morning the *poubelles* are duly emptied by the city's sanitation men. The smooth efficiency of this municipal service is due to the compulsory collaboration of the citizens—the *poubelle* may not be ignored—and if this is remarkable it is even more remarkable that this systemistic innovation has taken eighty years to cross the Alps and to be adopted in Rome. The municipality began to enforce it only in 1970.

This suggests that in the field of refuse disposal, as in so many other fields, systems are not invariably run in the best and most modern ways. It may seem trite to anyone who recalls the piles of refuse accumulating in the streets of London and Rome not so long ago—breakdowns due principally, though not exclusively, to sanitation men's strikes, and symptomatic of deep-seated and more serious failures. For we should note here, incidentally, that a critical estimate of a public system or service cannot exclude or ignore basic considerations. The efficiency of workers depends in part on their conditions of work, and if their reaction to those conditions is sullen trade-union hostility and strikes, the efficiency of the service suffers and the service itself may come to a halt.

In the United States—and recently in Europe to an appreciable extent—the limited efficiency of services for the collection and disposal of refuse has led to the use of kitchen waste grinders on an ever increasing scale. Built into the kitchen sink, they grind and pulverize domestic waste into small particles that are flushed down the drain. This method of elimination requires a fairly abundant supply of water. As a result, the domestic demand for water goes up and the problem of supplying water to large cities becomes even more acute than it was before. This is one more example of the way in which inefficiency in one system (city sanitation) can cause or aggravate a crisis in another system (water supply).

The supply of water—which includes its storage and distribution—is one of the large systems that is least subject to rational and ordered control. Though the domestic waste of water is well known, either the fight against it is halfhearted and weak—witness the publicity campaigns in the United States against dripping taps—or it is officially accepted, and nothing is done about it. For instance, in Rome, each consumer may have 1,000 liters of the Acqua Pia a day, either on tap or in a storage tank; when the tank is full, the supply is not cut off, and the water runs to waste in the sewers. Along with this waste goes, of course, the cities' enormous and growing demand for water. Larger and larger areas in country places have to be flooded with water (the broad valleys of the Catskills, for example) to serve as reservoirs for megalopolis.

Pollution has been a fashionable concern for some years now, and the term covers much more than the garbage, dirt, and litter familiar to a city sanitation squad. There is urgent debate about damage to the environment caused by industrial waste, about the pollution of the atmosphere (of which smog is but one example), and pollution of the water; rivers and lakes are now dying, in the sense that they no longer witness the reproduction of vegetable and animal life. The evidence abounds.

Now, there can be no doubt about the damage inflicted on the environment by industry; in a nation technologically advanced the yearly volume of industrial waste, solid and liquid, comes to tens of millions of cubic yards. But the gravity of the problem is differently assessed by different interests. J. Paul Austin, chairman of the board of the Coca-Cola Company, maintains that if industrial waste is not limited, rationalized, and made innocuous, the United States will soon be transformed into a huge graveyard. Coca-Cola has already made a modest contribution toward lessening the damage caused by the flood of waste products: it has installed grinding machines near supermarkets so that nonreturnable glass bottles may be pulverized to produce sand for children's playgrounds. The Reynolds Metals Company has started a scheme whereby empty aluminum cans may be collected and used again: it pays half a cent each for them. At the other extreme there are industrialists who maintain that any move to tighten legislation with more strenuous restrictions, forcing industry to accept responsibility for the harm done by its waste products, would be intolerable at a time when the economy is passing through a difficult phase, and the nation's industry must be able to meet foreign competition. This attitude—myopic to say the least—is strongly supported, for example, by representatives of the paper industry, which is notorious for producing stinking waste in large quantities and dumping it into rivers.

The dilemma is mercilessly real because the menace of industrial and urban waste will worsen steadily. But will it? Only on the hypothesis that industrial development, population increase, and the growing size of industrial systems are to continue undisturbed indefinitely.

In my view, industrial pollution presents a grave rather than an immediate problem because its consequences move at a slower tempo. It certainly causes the destruction of natural resources and an ecological imbalance; but these are not the most critical facts influencing the crises that can develop quickly and simultaneously in densely con-

centrated urban systems. Their relevance will become
much more urgent, of course, if such concentrations get
worse, as present industrial and urban areas penetrate one
another and a situation of wobbling instability manages
to maintain itself without actually precipitating a grave
crisis.

The short-term consequences of piles of refuse in the
streets will be simpler and deadlier than those of industrial
waste: the raw materials are not lacking—in any large
metropolis the yearly volume of collected refuse runs into
scores of millions of cubic yards. Ideas for a successful
industrial processing of urban waste—such as compressing
refuse into compact and resilient blocks for making new
roads—have not had much success up to now; nor is modern technology in this field providing quick and effective
solutions. Some years ago even a fine modern company
such as Honeywell was unsuccessful with their electronic
surveillance system for the sewer network in Sacramento
County, California. It comprised flow meters, analyzers,
recorders, integrators, and a large luminous display panel
that was to have monitored any fault occurring in the
whole setup. But it was a failure.

It is improbable that a deteriorating system of refuse
disposal would cause a multiple crisis in urban systems.
What is certain is the reverse of this. In a crisis involving
several other urban systems—such as electricity, transportation, and water—the further crisis in the disposal of refuse
becomes unavoidable. The rapid pile-up of garbage, etc.,
in city streets will aggravate the disorder already present
(taking away even more lanes from traffic already congested, for example). It will also produce new crises, such

as fires started by well-intentioned but inexperienced citizens who try to get rid of the stinking heaps in the streets by burning them. It will make the diffusion of illness and epidemics easier by giving new sources of food to rats and increasing their mobility and range. All such distresses are cumulative, in that all who are involved in the rapid breakdown of systems in quick succession become nervous and less efficient, and are themselves that much nearer to breakdown.

X

Death of the City of New York

John Doe lives in New York City, and he is convinced by now that the next ten years will be very much worse than the last ten.

He has been held up in traffic jams lasting for hours many times. A couple of times he had to abandon the car, making his way home on foot. Then, at night, he had to set out again to retrieve the car and drive it home.

He has sometimes been left without electricity for a few hours. Not that the consequences were very serious: some of the food in the refrigerator spoiled, and he had to drink two tepid martinis. Having to climb lots of stairs on foot was no fun, though; and in the morning he couldn't shave because his three razors are all electric.

Another thing, not untypical: There was a delay of five hours when he last flew to Boston. The flight should have taken just fifty minutes: a day's work lost.

It sometimes happens that the telephone is somehow out of order, and he cannot make contact with his business associates. Cut off and frustrated in this way, he misses good opportunities and loses a certain amount of money.

John Doe has his worries. With all this drug addiction he is anxious about his boys. Then there is inflation, and the slump on the stock exchange—and the menace of a nuclear war. The bills to be paid are an enduring headache, of course, not to mention the mortgage. Admittedly, he has little real information to go on as to whether these probabilities will actually affect him personally, and he has not done much to prepare for the crisis that he more than half expects—though he did buy a couple of candles, ten cans of frankfurters, and twenty cans of beer. (He has drunk practically all the beer.)

And yet the probability that a crisis is on the way is strong and growing stronger, in New York and in all great cities where people are densely concentrated. Here is one of the ways in which apocalypse could come, and megalopolis could die.

It can all begin with the simple coincidence of two traffic standstills, one on the roads and the other on the railways: a simultaneous paralysis of automobiles and trains. As a result, the next shift of air traffic controllers for two large airports are held up, and they fail to arrive. The previous shift, therefore, must stay on duty. These controllers usually work ten hours a day, six days a week. They have to follow two planes a minute on the radar screen, steering them when they take off and when they land, so that collisions may be avoided. After being at work continuously for nineteen hours in the control tower of O'Hare Airport in Chicago, one controller's ability to concentrate is much reduced; but as he is dead tired he does not realize this.

At length he makes a grave error, and a 707 about to land collides with a DC-9 that has just taken off. The two planes, tangled together, hit a high-voltage line and break it. The electric load on the broken line is instantly distributed over other lines, but they are already overloaded. The automatic protection devices go into operation, therefore, and with a chain reaction the entire electric network of Illinois, Michigan, Ohio, Pennsylvania, New York, Connecticut, and Massachusetts loses the synchronism and goes out of service. But this time the blackout is a long one; it will last for many days.

The time is January. The temperature is below zero. It is beginning to snow again, and the snow plows cannot function because the streets are blocked by cars. Many cars use up all their gasoline, keeping the engine running uselessly. Refueling is impossible because the electric motors of the gasoline pumps cannot function. Many drivers abandon their cars and thereby add to the traffic tangle.

Since the trains are not running, many city workers are forced to camp in their offices, where they try to keep warm by lighting fires. Many of these will get out of control, setting buildings ablaze. The fires cannot be extinguished because the fire engines cannot reach them through streets solidly encumbered with cars. A few thousand people die as scenes of panic ensue.

The freezing dawn of the following day finds the situation unchanged. Fifteen million people are virtually abandoned without supplies and without information. As they all try to telephone, the entire network is blocked. Many people try to reach their homes or friends on foot, setting off on marches of some dozen miles or so which they do not succeed in completing. Many of them die in the snow. Others ask for shelter where there is none to give, and either meet with violence or resort to it. Firearms are used—several thousands of the tens of millions of fire-arms in the possession of private citizens in the United States.

But what of all the elaborate municipal provisions for emergencies of this kind? The answer is that the paralysis of transportation puts them out of action and prevents civil defense workers and volunteers from reaching their posts.

During the second day a state of emergency is pro-claimed, and the armed forces assume all civil powers. The paralysis of the airports makes it impossible to use air bridges for the supplies that cannot go by road or rail. Army helicopters try to meet the need, but their capacity is quickly seen to be unequal to it.

On the third day the looting of supermarkets begins, and troops try to stop it. There are riots and a few hundred people are killed.

John Doe becomes aware that he is totally unprepared for this kind of situation. The two candles are finished and all the electric appliances that fill his house are useless.

José Gutierez, the Puerto Rican, finds his situation not so bad. His subsistence level being very low anyhow, he is not especially distressed at what is happening. He has never had a telephone and is accustomed to having the electricity cut off because his payments are often in arrears. His home, with its bare minimum of necessities, corresponds to his primitive way of living. He is accustomed to a competitive and even violent existence. It will be José who will clobber John Doe—and survive—when they fight for cylinders of liquid gas.

The number of such deaths from violence, however, will be far exceeded by deaths from cold and hunger. The total casualty list will include a remarkable number of deaths in hospitals. Some millions of people will die in the two weeks during which the crisis will last. Then things will begin to move again, but revival will be slow and will take place on very much lower levels than before.

The elimination of atmospheric pollution—one advantage that the standstill of power stations, industries, and internal combustion engines will bring—will seem a disadvantage, too, as survivors face the impossible and attempt the timely removal of millions of corpses: they will prefer the old smog.

With hygiene virtually absent, an epidemic will be the widespread new phenomenon, causing more deaths. This will be the decisively lethal fact: half of the surviving population will die of bubonic plague. Historians estimate that in the fourteenth century the plague destroyed between half and two thirds of the population of Europe; but that is far away and long ago, and we cannot help thinking that plague is one of history's horrors, unknown to the modern world for about 170 years. But as Hans Zinsser has written in his book *Rats, Lice and History*:

We have no satisfactory explanation for the disappearance of plague epidemics from the Western countries, and we must assume that in spite of the infectiousness of the plague-bacillus, the plentifulness of rats, their occasional infection with plague and their invariable infestation with fleas, the evolution of an epidemic requires a delicate adjustment of many conditions which have fortunately failed to eventuate in Western Europe and America during the last [nineteenth] century. The most reasonable clue lies in the increased domestication of rats. Plague epidemics in man are usually preceded by widespread epizootics among rats; and, under the conditions of housing, food storage, cellar construction, and such that have gradually developed in civilized countries, rats do not migrate through cities and villages as they formerly did. . . . Plague foci among rats remain restricted to individual families and colonies.

Zinsser wrote in 1935; since then antibiotics have become available. This new fact—with proper hygienic controls operating normally through the supply-and-distribution systems of modern society—could undoubtedly strangle a new epidemic at birth. But an urban crisis such as I have outlined above could have just that ecological imbalance that would unleash plague; it would perpetuate conditions of disorganization and want that would allow the lethal horror to continue undisturbed.

Today our ecologists utter cries of alarm because the equilibrium of our planet is being disturbed. They warn us against the destruction of whole species of animals; against pollution; against the increase of carbon dioxide in the atmosphere, with a resulting slow rise in its temperature. But John Doe's crisis will find them facing a menace much more deadly, direct, and swift than anything that the evils of pollution promise. When this menace is recognized as such, it will be too late.

Urban crisis will not be exclusive to New York; that particular megalopolis serves as our example of what will occur in every great metropolitan city. On the other hand, the vivid events here foreshadowed would not produce the dark age overnight; they would be, rather, the germinal beginning—the loosening, disintegrating agent—of a profound breakdown of society and of civilization itself as we know it.

People of all cultures have never been willing merely to endure disasters: they have always looked for someone or something to blame—even when the cause was drought, tempest, flood, or hurricane. Their scapegoats have been individuals, such as Jonah; or communities, such as Jews; or categories gratuitously labeled, such as "witches"; or neighboring peoples. Sometimes they have been concepts, often anthropomorphic, of totems, demons, or gods whose anger was deemed to be the cause of current troubles.

As recently as 1965 many Americans believed that their November blackout had been the deliberate work of communists or anarchists. No savageries were perpetrated as a result of these obsessions, but they might have been. After a terrible catastrophe, witch hunts can take terribly violent forms, in comparison with which Senator Joseph McCarthy's probes, charges, and persecutions would look as harmless as a charade at a party. Innocent people may be killed, even burned at the stake—the latest additions to history's unfinished toll of sacrificial victims. The guiltless will live in fear of smear tactics and gratuitous accusations. The phobia of sabotage will give a further twist to the mentality of the accuser. Not only the foreigner but the fellow citizen will become an object of suspicion. In short, society will lose its cohesion and stability as the wounds of the disaster fester more deeply.

The ability to organize and to look ahead—not very efficiently, it may be—is a driving force in the ongoing life of a society; but this becomes almost useless when confronted with realities strange to the experience and the memory of all living people. They do things that are useless or harmful, in the pathetic attempt to fit the old shape of things, which they cannot forget or disown, to the new shape of things, which they have to accept and make the best of. For some time there is stagnation, with no one able to see a working, forward-looking model for the future in any surviving system, much less in the supersystem constituted by the whole of society.

But it is obvious that "the whole of society," as we think of it today, would not survive as a supersystem. It would become fragmented into smaller systems, with but little intercommunication. These would have a certain self-sufficiency and stability. Such feudalism is another trait that future conditions would have in common with those of the Dark and Middle Ages (say, A.D. 450 to 1450); and we may expect that, once again, drastic diminutions of population in the most densely inhabited areas of the earth would produce huge displacements or migrations of people. These would happen primarily as flight from areas struck by catastrophe; and if plague were rampant, it would quicken their speed. Later people would reoccupy the areas now almost uninhabited—desirable as resettlement areas because of the free availability of houses and artifacts in abundance.

It is difficult to foresee what the character and vicissitudes of these movements of people would be. Most of them would probably be on a small scale and over short distances, oscillating around some center once inhabited as metropolis or megalopolis.

But there could be momentous movements of population, on the other hand, over very long distances, as the people of the so-called third world enter the area occupied by what would be left of modern Western civilization. Sooner or later there would emerge from such a whirlpool of collisions new and profound possibilities—the earnest of the future renaissance. It is probable, indeed, that the great drop in population—widespread among the advanced nations of modern Western civilization during their coming dark age—would be relatively small in the countries of the third world, where there would be a less phenomenal growth of instability, a fact that would be virtually equivalent to greater stability.

It could happen, for example, that China would not experience a breakdown in its systems simultaneously with those of the Western world. The present direction of Chinese development suggests that this is probable. If so, the Chinese might be expected to expand beyond their borders, first toward the territories of the Soviet Union and then throughout the rest of the world.

It is conceivable that the currents of thought and the ideologies of the Chinese revolution, or of the movements that it has inspired, will have effects—weak and remote perhaps—on the development of this renaissance that will follow the coming dark age, just as the traditions started by shamans among the Huns, when they were still very far from Europe, may have been transmitted through migrations and clashes of populations and cultures and may have had some influence on the humanism of the Renaissance five centuries ago.

I have been elaborating tragic hypotheses. In chapter XVII I mention ways—not very likely to succeed, I think —in which we might try to prevent them from coming true.

One might maintain, *sub specie aeternitatis*, that whatever is, is best; that we live in the best of all possible worlds, and that it is not unfitting that our civilization should collapse to give place to something new and more efflorescent in the more or less distant future. From this point of view, should we be any more entitled to complain than were those who lived through the decline and fall of the Roman Empire fifteen centuries ago? Only if we believe that the progress and the developments achieved during our past five centuries have led to something better than the achievement of the Greeks and the Romans. And if we can give no more optimistic an answer than this, our situation is truly dramatic.

XI

Is Modern War Irrelevant to the Issue?

Only a few optimists are content with the world as it is: they have too little imagination to see it as it might be. On the other hand, very many people want to change it, and believe that the most important immediate task is to bring down the System: it is the prime obstacle to all improvement. Indeed, its very existence is the most serious evil of all. There are others who also object to the world as it is and would certainly like to destroy its economic system and its power structures, but they hold that the most threatening danger is the destruction of our planet by a new world war, that nuclear disarmament is the one thing needed, and the first objective.

There are two theses here, and before going on to examine in subsequent chapters the more remote causes of the coming breakdown of the great systems, and to speculate on what will happen after it is complete, I want to devote this chapter and the next to a discussion of these two theses which, for brevity's sake, I will call respectively disarmament and protest. In this chapter I shall argue that modern warfare, despite its huge destructive power, is really irrelevant to the main issue.

If the fear that a great world war may break out is, in fact, justifiable, it is reasonable to get the priorities right. That is, to worry first and foremost about averting the destruction of the great systems. Preventing their breakdown is a secondary anxiety that may be deferred.

Perhaps there are no substitutes for war. During the twentieth century there have been many proposals for abolishing armed conflicts and substituting international arbitration. Of the organizations born of such proposals, the League of Nations did not serve to prevent the wars in Abyssinia and Spain or World War II; and the United Nations has been ineffective over the war in Korea, the war in Vietnam, the war between Israel and the Arab countries, the war between Biafra and Nigeria—and over other uses of armed force, speedier and more efficient, such as the Russian interventions in Hungary and Czechoslovakia.

In his book *The Culture of Cities*, Lewis Mumford has sought to establish a general theory about the tragic effects of war on the excessive and disordered development of large cities. From the primitive stage of *eopolis*, a simple aggregate of people, the city passed first to the stage of *polis* and then to that of mother city, *metropolis*. The inescapable process of expansion leads the metropolis to become *megalopolis*, where growing disorganization produces the false and fatal solution of dictatorship. This is *tyrannopolis*. To maintain their position of power, dictators incite the people to war or force them into imperialist warfare which—along with want and disease—finally destroys the cities, bringing them to their last and definitive stage, *necropolis*.

It is curious that when this book was reissued after World War II Mumford made the emphatic claim that the first edition of 1936 had been prophetic, as demonstrated by the destruction wrought by war on Warsaw, London, Stalingrad, Nuremberg, Berlin, Frankfurt, Leningrad, Rotterdam, and, of course, Hiroshima and Nagasaki. Today, twenty-five years afterward, all these cities have been rebuilt. Not only that: they are now the scenes of urban congestion, forcefully demonstrating that even modern warfare is powerless to restrain the growth of systems. We reach the same conclusions if we examine the graph of world population from 1850 to 1950. From 1850 to 1900 the population of the world grew from 1,150 to 1,650 millions (a 43 per cent increase); in the second half-century the increase was 44 per cent, from 1,650 to 2,350 millions—despite the world wars, the effects of which are scarcely noticeable on the graph.

It is instructive to look at a comparison in tabular form of the countries involved in the war—their populations in 1935 and in 1966, and the losses they sustained during the war years. (The figures represent millions.)

	Population 1935	Losses 1939–45	Population 1966
U.S.A.	137.0	1.04	196.0
U.S.S.R.	162.0	13.50	236.0
Japan	84.0	6.50	100.0
Germany	66.0	9.50	77.0
Britain	45.0	0.57	55.0

	Population 1935	Losses 1939–45	Population 1966
France	41.0	0.75	50.0
Italy	41.0	0.35	52.0
Poland	32.0	5.60	32.0
Czechoslovakia	14.5	0.50	14.2
Yugoslavia	14.0	1.70	20.0
Totals	636.5	40.01	832.2

Despite the wartime death of 6.4 per cent of the populations here considered, the total population of these same countries increased by 31 per cent in the thirty years from 1935 to 1966. This means that their demographic expansion (or population explosion) was not slowed down appreciably even by the greatest war in which humanity has ever engaged.

But there is another consideration that is even more important. In his 1948 paper "Military and Political Consequences of Atomic Energy," Patrick M. S. Blackett proved that the bombings of urban areas during World War II had almost negligible military effects. For example, the bombings of Hamburg in the summer of 1943 killed more than 60,000 people; but they had the further effect of lowering the standard of living in the city and greatly reducing the demand for personnel employed in various urban services. As a result, the difficulty that had plagued industry in that area—lack of labor—was largely eliminated; and within five months Hamburg had recovered 80 per cent of its previous productive capacity. It was not the destruction of cities but the precision bombing of transportation systems that brought about the collapse of German industrial production.

At this point it can certainly be argued that the nuclear stockpiles of the great—and, now, of the not so great—powers suffice for the annihilation of several nations, and perhaps of the human race itself. This is now defined as overkill (i.e., every adversary wiped out). But would a nuclear holocaust, made possible by the capacity for overkill now acquired by the U.S.A. and the U.S.S.R., substantially change our picture of the foreseeable future of civilization? There are three main hypotheses to be considered.

The first hypothesis—the destruction of the whole or almost the whole of the human race—is certainly the worst from every point of view. It dismisses the problems that we are investigating by wiping out the civilization of which they are the tragic expression. In short, the consequences of this horrible hypothesis are so final that it is useless and meaningless to pause over them. (This does not mean that we need not try to prevent the hypothesis—the indiscriminate and generalized use of nuclear bombing—from becoming a reality. Any movement advocating disarmament or the prohibition of nuclear weapons must be supported. But the forms that such support should take, and the hopes and probabilities of their success, have nothing to do with my immediate argument.)

The second hypothesis is that nuclear arms will never be used, thanks to this very fear of total destruction: nations will continue to make war with conventional weapons as they do at present. This is not improbable: it has a well-known precedent in the fact that during World War

II no nation used poison gas. But as we have seen, the number of people destroyed in conventional warfare is trifling and negligible in comparison with the giant dimensions and implications of the main problem. So that this second possibility cannot command our most urgent concern. If it were verified with the passage of time, it could at most keep the real problem at arm's length for some years, and so delay the final instability and collapse toward which the large systems would still be moving.

The third, the only relevant hypothesis, is that of an atomic war which, in a very brief period of time, would reduce the population of the world by 1 or 2 billion people. It seems improbable that this could happen, since, to bring it about, the number of nuclear bombings and the places selected as targets would have to be calibrated with the greatest accuracy. But the objective of the strategists on each side of the conflict would be the classic one of inflicting maximum hurt; and this would lead to mass killings, widespread and far from calibrated. There is one fact that might notably limit the number of such deaths. The inefficiency and uncontrollability of large systems is no peculiarity of civil life; it is familiar in military systems, too. There is no excluding the possibility, therefore, that despite their intent to kill off a great part of the human race, military men will succeed only in destroying a few hundred million people—a billion at most. The resulting state of things would be very like what we have already conjectured—the halving of the population of the advanced nations, since the targets of most of the nuclear missiles would be concentrated in these countries.

For all systemistic purposes, therefore, the hypothesis

of a new world war is a variant—not a strikingly significant one—of other hypotheses that have already been put forward. The events that it anticipates would certainly be no limiting factor preventing large systems from degenerating into instability and initiating a new dark age. This still looks like the eventual tragedy; and its probability steadily grows, independently of whether there is war or peace in the world.

XII

The Futility of Protest

On August 7, 1934, the football team from Dundalk in the Republic of Ireland played an away match against Banbridge in Ulster. They came by train and sensed an atmosphere of Protestant hostility from the moment they arrived. During the match tempers were high and play was rough. It had rained, and the ground was soft. Covered with mud and bruises, the Catholics returned to their dressing room having lost 5–1. They were accompanied to the station by a small crowd anxious to exult to the very last moment over their defeated opponents. As the train began to move southward, a voice from the platform shouted, "They will be grinding their teeth tonight in the Vatican."

The basic assumption here—that Pius XI was kept continuously posted with the minutest detail of every Catholic/Protestant confrontation through a notoriously ramified network of Jesuits and Catholic activists—is not more absurd than the supposition of many an opponent of the System today as he inveighs against the power of big industry, which never fails to oppress the worker at every level, and to regiment and enslave the masses.

It is not easy to give a brief and relevant account of what contemporary protest really means, since the point of view of its exponents is hard to discover. Their writings provide no definition of terms used; there are gratuitous transitions and jumps in the argument; and an attention to fact is certainly no part of it. Interpretation of their ideas can be little more than hypothetical, therefore.

Those who contest the rightness of almost everything are not easily challenged, partly because they express themselves badly, but mainly because their ideas change very quickly and they soon go out of fashion. A short time after Herbert Marcuse had put together his pastiches of Hegel, Marx, and Freud, Charles Reich tried to surpass him by inventing the Conscience III label for those who have been set free, who follow every instinct, who smoke marijuana and refuse responsibility. The fashionable idiom for a month or two was the "greening of America" as imagined by Reich. But someone else is always preparing a new recipe to push the Charles Reichs to one side, to offer new liberations, vaster and more intuitive truths—but equally arbitrary.

The position of protesters is publicized and known well enough. According to them, an industrialized society is really an establishment of fear which forces the majority of the people to perform tasks that estrange and alienate. Even when the powerful do nothing directly violent, their propaganda eliminates all possibility of free choice, since the alternatives presented are illusory, having the sole purpose of keeping the System functioning. The contribution of cybernetics and computers is to make human enslavement total.

This way of seeing things is properly characteristic of drop-outs; that is, those who have put themselves outside the system and have ceased to go to college or to work. To call them Maoists would be inappropriate, since real Maoists are not found among them. In fact, even among those who do wear this label the fundamental principles of the Chinese revolution are not found—only traces of them. Those principles may be summarized as: the use of reason and the habit of rational discussion; the primacy of education, particularly scientific and technical education; the protection and development of industrialization; increased productivity; better organization, not only political and ideological, but also in accountancy, management, and productivity; military discipline, not only for tactical purposes, but based on the concept of the soldier as peasant, technician, and student. True Maoists, then, would set themselves definite short-term and long-term aims, and among these would certainly be the maintenance of industrial plants and the entire production system at their full efficiency.

The attitude of drop-outs is the polar opposite of this. They maintain that questions of organization, actual concrete problems, and specific plans devised to satisfy the needs of humanity in the mass are all irrelevant. That freedom from industrial discipline in fact lowers productivity and reduces millions of people to misery in consequence is, for them, unimportant. If a society lacks technicians who have been forced to become efficient by training, study, and examination, the immediate result will be the technical incompetence of the squads in charge of vital enterprises, and the further result will be large-scale disaster and death. Drop-outs deny this logical inevitability: to them the destruction of the System is the only thing that matters.

The destruction would begin by denying certain necessities, such as the struggle for existence, the need to earn one's living, the principles of efficiency, competition and productivity, and the discipline of the instincts. This destruction of basic necessities would then be accompanied by destructive action, threatening authority and so bringing peace. The final goal would be the reign of liberty. The development of new biological necessities would be requisite for this: so would a theory of man that would give rise to a new morality—the successor and destroyer of Judaic-Christian morality, freeing sexual activity from repression, and assuring privacy, calm, beauty, and "unmerited" happiness to everyone.

Now, it is a good norm of mental hygiene that we should choose the job that we like doing and that both amuses and interests us. But this simple principle, certainly relevant when personal choices have to be made, is inadequate if applied generally to the dilemmas of whole populations. This ideal of making work desirable in itself apparently has been made a reality in the People's Republic of China and in Japan, apart from all awkward questions about working hours and payment. In the Far East however the right result was obtained in the right way; that is, by means of the stimulus of adequate motivation rather than by vague declarations about the end being desirable in itself.

These aspirations might be thought religious because

of their disinterestedness, and also because many of those who cherish them expect liberation to come from an armed prophet who will destroy the powerful and protect the weak—a good dictator for the guidance of waverers. There is no escaping the fact that the messiah expected by the people of protest is strikingly like the strong man desired by reactionaries.

The resemblances between authoritarian movements and some of these movements of protest are not accidental. Both types have, in fact, a common anti-intellectual basis, affirming the supremacy of action over theory, and over thought in general. They prefer being violent to being convincing; they go in for a romantic veneration of youth. The intuitions of certain drop-outs resemble those of Hitler rather than those of Henri Bergson. The very name "counterculture" recalls the notorious words of Goebbels: "When I hear the word 'culture' I reach for my pistol."

But the most serious fault of the people of protest is their naïveté. Their belief in huge prearranged and harmful designs that they attribute to a complex of commercial, industrial, and military interests is just false. If such designs do exist, they may certainly be pronounced execrable, but not evidence of efficient planning. I have been describing large systems getting out of control—a hard objective fact indicating that the actual involutions of developed societies are not premeditatively willed by anyone. Our involvement in them is random and unordered, and this very fact means that the system would break down and end of itself, even though it sustained no attacks from outside.

It is strange that those who devote most of their energies to listing and criticizing the defects of contemporary society have failed to consider its greatest defect: its systemistic deficiency and frailty.

If new social structures in the future are to have a real hope of developing and lasting, their systemistic aspects will have to be studied afresh and their statistical problems solved rationally. It is a necessity that presses with equal weight on the old structures and on the new: unless there is rationalization, the former cannot survive, and the latter cannot even begin to exist.

But it is just here that the most complete void is found. No one has put forward plans or projects for raising the standard of life for large masses of people, making the time available (of both teachers and taught) for educating the masses to higher and higher levels, and at the same time keeping efficiency high and increasing productivity. Ideological preoccupations prevent people from even suspecting the existence of systemistic problems. It seems that the technico-scientific notions of protest movements derive from textbooks at least a century old. But during the last hundred years several things have happened, both in the field of pure science and in that of technology and industrial organization. And to interpret the actual world as if it were that of Thomas Alva Edison, with the addition of a few million TV sets, cars, and somewhat larger industrial plants, hardly is conducive to understanding contemporary reality.

It would not be worth bothering with the statements and theories of the people of protest were it not that their very numbers must have some importance, and may accelerate appreciably the breakdown of the large systems. Their indirect influence is perceptible in the growing percentage of drop-outs among the young. This reduces recruitment of technicians and other professional men, and is responsible, according to many industrialists, for a decreasing productivity in their respective enterprises.

Direct action—such as riots, strikes, street barricades, the occupation of universities, factories, and public buildings—can paralyze the life of a whole nation, as happened in France in May 1968. It has been estimated that the French economy needed a whole year in which to recover from the losses sustained in those months of paralysis.

These subversive activities, however, are usually no more than episodes: they are incapable of leading to revolutions in the true and full sense because there is no careful planning beforehand. Good revolutionaries have to be good planners too. Odon Pohr, who was a minister in Béla Kun's revolutionary government in Budapest for a short time, used to say that in every coup d'état there comes a moment in which success or failure depends on whether or not an appropriate set of rubber stamps is available.

There is no need to believe in a huge international conspiracy co-ordinating student unrest at Berkeley and the Sorbonne, in Berlin and Rome, in order to give to the phenomena of protest the features of a large system. Nor may one speak of a breakdown of this system, since it has never made the grade in any appreciable sense and seems unlikely to do so.

Protesters, then, will hardly succeed in creating a new society, though they might succeed, in certain cases, in delivering the fatal blow to systems already beginning to collapse. Yet even here their likelihood of success is fairly small. In July 1970 the underground paper *East Village Other* published the following manifesto:

> *Be the first in your block to help blow out the*
> *electric power network of the North East*

East Village Other is proud to announce the first annual blackout of the Werewolves which is fixed for 3 p.m. on Wednesday, August 19, 1970. Once more let us put the system to the test. Switch on all the electric equipment you can lay hands on. Help the companies producing and distributing electric power to improve their balance sheets by consuming as much power as you can; and even then find some way of using a bit more. In particular, switch on electric heaters, toasters, air conditioning, and any other apparatus with a high consumption. Refrigerators turned up to the maximum, with their doors left open, can cool down a large apartment in an amusing way.* After an afternoon's consumption-spree we will meet in Central Park to bay at the moon.

Tune in! Plug in! Blow out!

Hospitals and other emergency services are hereby warned, and invited to take necessary precautions.

In reality, there was no blackout on August 19, 1970, and that particular group of protest-makers merely demon-

---

* This is not so. If a refrigerator is switched on and its door is left open, the temperature of the room in which it stands goes up, not down.

strated its inefficacy. On the other hand, a blackout of four hours did take place in New York in February 1971 without anyone's having preconceived or planned it.

Such an extra consumption of electric power to express annoyance could have no decisive effect, not even in the future, if the systems had the solid steadiness requisite for survival, let alone for growth. But they lack this reliability. Protesters could spare their pains if they reflected that the hated system is collapsing by itself.

Understanding a very complicated process, whether it be natural or man-made, requires really hard work; but understanding is made easier by the logic implicit in the fact that the process works, and that in it there are numerous sequences of causes and effects. It is much more difficult to understand why a complicated process ceases to work: to diagnose the pathological condition, a knowledge of physiology is needed.

These considerations explain the error into which certain ill-equipped revolutionaries are liable to fall. They know that in the advanced nations of the West men of learning give an honored place to logic and rationality; and also to economy—either in the sense of frugality or in the sense of "economics," the optimum use of the forces able to achieve certain purposed ends. The revolutionaries realize, however, that the results are unsatisfactory and they therefore blame the formal principles of conventional wisdom for the prevailing instabilities, breakdowns, inefficiencies, waste, injustices, oppressions, inequalities, and decadence; and they conclude that better results could be obtained simply by standing these civilized principles on their heads and cultivating what is irresponsible, illogical, and makeshift. They fail to see that the blemishes that mark the actions and omissions of the conservers are, in fact, the enemy that they should be attacking.

It seems that the Chinese Communists have not fallen into this error. If they alone are to prove immune, they may well deserve to inherit the scepter of the empires that have fallen.

XIII

The Crisis of Management

James Burnham was a bad prophet. His forecasts of Nazi victory and Soviet expansion were invalidated within a very few years of their formulation; and even the title of his book, *The Managerial Revolution,* which made so much noise thirty years ago, seems badly mistaken today. *The Managerial Involution* would have been better.

For the widespread mismanagement of enterprises large and small is an absolute fact. It is denied by company directors, but its truth should be clear from the evidence I have already given. Further, it is a sorry truth that is indirectly confirmed by numerous squibs and wisecracks of recent years: Parkinson's Law; the Peter Principle on reaching the unavoidable level of incompetence; and, much more seriously, Robert Townsend's *Up the Organization.* It would be trite to say that such skits contain inaccuracies and exaggerations; they would hardly entertain us if they did not. But they would not amuse us either, if the airs and inefficiencies which they mock did not in fact exist. Townsend, for example, states bluntly that in the

United States there are 6,001 corporations and that, of these, 6,000 are incompetently managed. (He explains that Nader's Raiders is the one exception, an organization for the defense of consumers and the public, the founder of which—Ralph Nader—became famous because of his attacks on General Motors.) Now, if it were not true that, say, at least half of these corporations *are* poorly directed, Townsend's dictum would not raise even a smile; it would simply be the outburst of a paranoiac.

One of the institutions deemed to be organized with an iron (some would say "premeditated") efficiency is the Pentagon. It is instructive, therefore, to read the findings of a report drawn up in 1970 by a committee of fourteen leading industrialists, among whom were the presidents of the Metropolitan Life Insurance Company, Thompson-Ramo-Woodridge, Teledyne-Ryan-Aeronautical, and the Caterpillar Tractor Company. Commissioned by President Nixon, they labored for a year, analyzing and criticizing the operation of America's supreme military machine. They reported that

• there are 35,000 employees too many at the Pentagon, chiefly employed in making out passes
• billions of dollars are spent every year in the fruitless attempt to make armed forces function in ways that are basically mistaken
• contracts signed by the Defense Department are too large, and all the procedures of military acquisitions should be completely revised and modified
• the excessively centralized organization of the Penta-

gon often prevents any decisions whatever from being made.

The president of the committee, G. W. Fitzhugh, said in an interview: "We have not found personnel problems, but problems of organization. The astonishing thing is that anything works at all." This state of things could certainly explain many of the American failures in Vietnam.

In recent decades average managerial ability has probably remained fairly constant, but it has not been able to match the enlarged dimensions of its problems. If we bear in mind the levels of the gross national product of various nations at the beginning of the century and today, and if we compare the aims that were realized seventy years ago (such as railway systems, or the metropolitan subways of Paris, London, and New York) with their present-day counterparts, contemporary management hardly shows to advantage. We have already referred to the almost incredible fact that in the United States the BART system, which is to serve San Francisco, Oakland, and the cities on the Bay, is the first system of rapid urban transport to have been planned and implemented since 1908.

There are notable exceptions, such as certain IRI projects that have been realized in Italy (the autostrada system, the new steel plants, etc.); but in the large majority of cases dissatisfaction is fully justified.

In these few paragraphs about mismanagement I am not pretending to dictate specific rules—a theory of the subject—for the use of managers, but only to justify my pessimism as to whether the process of degeneration in the great systems can possibly be halted **and** changed into a process of regeneration. If the managers who are available today are not equal to adopting conventional solutions (which I have called handbook solutions), there is little hope that they will be equal to inventing those new and exceptional solutions that are now indispensable.

The incompetence of managers is often hidden by the short-term successes of the organizations they control, successes that are due to favorable chance events. The main causes of this incompetence are: a lack of information (i.e., inability to gather and interpret current data, or ignorance of professional and technical methods); a lack of imagination; a lack of courage, a close adherence to a rule book because of inability to adapt oneself to changes in the real world, and to realize that no collection of rules covers every possible event in the future.

Defects of character have their relevance here, too. They are very often justified or rationalized as being due to strain, or alienation, or overwork, or even—in less sophisticated circles—to nervous exhaustion. As this book is no manual of psychotherapy, I drop this subject at once; but I want to make a personal suggestion to all who maintain that their characters are definitely formed by now and cannot be further modified. I advise them to read Bertrand Russell's *Conquest of Happiness*, a book written in 1930 but completely modern nevertheless. Also the texts of St. Ignatius Loyola, one of the greatest managers who ever lived, in his *Spiritual Exercises* and in the constitution that he drew up for the Jesuit Order. A book waits to be written on the science of management interpreted in the light of the theories and methods of St. Ignatius. It is my opinion that to reread St. Ignatius—having the problems of industrial organization and of labor in mind—will suggest principles and new solutions more significant than the rereading of Machiavelli will. Such a use of the author of *The Prince* has been tried, not very happily, by Burnham; and in a way that is much more entertaining, at least, by Antony Jay in his book *Management and Machiavelli*. There have been many others.

Confronted by the nonspecialists—Machiavelli, St. Ignatius, and Russell—contemporary writing on the science of management cuts a poor figure, as do articles that appear in specialist reviews, limited as they mostly are to general and obvious expositions, to classifications of little interest, or to applying very simple mathematical procedures to the settlement of issues that are usually unreal.

An exception deserving special notice is the article by Robert A. Frosch, assistant secretary to the Navy, entitled "A New Look at Systems Engineering."[7] Frosch simply asks that systems engineering be applied to systems engineering; that systems analysis be applied to systems analysis; and that techniques of management be applied to management itself. He presents the negative aspects of systems engineering today by insisting that responsibility must lie very largely with the managers who plan and run it. His critical points deserve orderly summary.

1. Many project managers are in a muddle between two worlds. A paper work world, consisting of all the documentation proper to a system and to procedures for follow-up as the system expands. And the real world constituted by the people on whom the effective working of the system depends. Disaster inevitably awaits the manager who spends his time in that central clearing house of in-

formation, his office, instead of in the places where the work is actually being done. The uninvolved are the uninformed, since the fait accompli is all that the nerve center of information will know about.

2. Techniques of control (such as PERT, or progress charts) ought not to be taken as literally as they sometimes are. They provide no more than a schematized version of reality; and those who would adhere to them too strictly would be turning their backs on indispensable features of real system-design and development. Such features may not follow from what was initially projected: as the project passes through its successive stages, they may emerge as modifications and improvements.

3. The techniques of forecasting can be a strait jacket. They impose *a priori* formulas settling how the system will work out in terms of performance, time, and costs. But it is a mistake to compare the empirical behavior of systems at work only with the forecasts initially made about them, and to deliver a favorable judgment if—and only if—behavior and forecasts coincide. We have to determine whether performance and effective costs satisfy what the system requires, not whether they conform to *a priori* formulas. This is the right criterion.

4. Systems ought not to be thought of as having only a static existence in space and an unchanging existence in time, but as existing in space-time; that is, easily modifiable and apt to require modifications, and so able to go on giving returns that will be useful and significant in the real world as it may show itself to be a long time ahead: a world, that is, that may differ notably from what it was in the past when the systems were planned.

5. A system has to have its specific characteristics, admittedly; but we must not forget that these can only constitute an abstract rather than an objectively real whole. It is a partial rather than a total description of what is aimed at. One can "realize" a system, therefore (or something that corresponds to its subtotal of specifications), and yet be very far from having a sensible solution to one's problem.

Anyone practically concerned with the problems inherent in systems (or more simply, perhaps, anyone with a little common sense) may feel that Frosch's criticisms are very obvious and are justified only if aimed at bad systems engineering. Frosch anticipates this very objection and writes: "Things are defined by what is done, not by what is said; and if what I am describing is bad system-engineering I can only add that I rarely see any other kind."

The same objection could be made to Frosch's proposals for improving things in the future. We ought to stop using our best men to draw up reports for their superiors, while there is no one attending the shop. Every big problem needs a competent man with good collaborators who can be relied on to understand its true nature—not just the particular scenario that someone has written, but what is in the mind of the men who decided the problem was to be solved.

One of the plainest tokens of the gravity of our situation is that though the foregoing criticisms and suggestions are obvious, they have to be made with dramatic emphasis to get anyone to heed them.

Aurelio Peccei is another manager who does not conform to type. In his recent book *The Chasm Ahead*[8] he writes: "My opinion as a manager is that as we face an extreme case of bad management—the present way in which human affairs are ordered—we will have to have recourse to meticulous verificatory research . . . and later, when the stage of decision and action is reached, to a good dose of refined techniques and of pragmatism."

Concrete action resulting from such research, according to Peccei, ought to take the form of emergency plans on a world scale, by all the advanced nations, including the United States and the Soviet Union. This is indispensable if "a big change of direction" is to be realized during the seventies. That such plans are indispensable is no guarantee, however, that they will be adopted; and it must be added that the commissioning of studies by committees of experts often masks an intention to do nothing. It is a way of delaying concrete decision. Further, Peccei's book was written in 1968; and though its basic analysis remains valid (according to which the whole of modern society is moving toward an era of disorder and crisis), the period that has elapsed since then has produced new facts that are clearly more alarming than those that provoked his cry of alarm. In fact, Peccei was particularly concerned with the technological gap between the United States and Europe, and with its consequences: the brain drain from Europe to America; the growing difficulties experienced by European firms because they are on too small a scale; the dissipation and waste of European resources on enterprises having no likelihood of success, with the result that resources needed for solving urgent problems are not available; Europe's growing technological lag behind the United States, for which its inadequate interest in research and development is to blame. What Peccei anticipated, therefore, was a growing gap between the United States (where progress would be accelerating at a uniform rate) and Europe (where there would be stagnation or regression). Europe's inability to match American success would give her an inferiority complex about technology which would do much to limit new enterprises and initiatives.

It is to be noticed, however, that the majority of the examples of breakdown that I have cited come from the United States itself. They occurred between 1965 and 1973. This is due to the fact that America's technological and managerial efficiency, though indisputably higher than Europe's, is insufficient to balance the greater seriousness of its dimensional problems and the instability that these involve. As for Europe, we should certainly expect that in terms of density and comparative mass the statistics of the waste, congestion, and crisis occurring there would be lower than in the United States.

Government action, or lack of action, will also leave its mark on the future. It is well known that government and public organizations in many countries are reduced to impotence, if not to paralysis, through their very inefficiency and the inadequacy of their directive staffs. This means that the decisions made by the politicians fail to get the action that would make them effective.

An illustrative case book is not my purpose. Apart from the inefficiency of the Pentagon, already mentioned, I will merely record President Nixon's proposal in April 1969 that NATO should devote at least part of its activities to the solution of civil problems (transportation in and between cities, ecology, water supply, etc.). Quite a few years have gone by but the authoritative proposal has not led to any concrete action. One could give an enormous number of Italian illustrations here. I limit myself to citing the interminable and often obscure discussions, accusations, and pronouncements about government *immobilismo* (inaction) and to stressing how symptomatic the coinage of this relatively new term is.

I have pointed to the problems of mismanagement as a remote cause of the dark age that is imminent, but we must not forget that this is also a continuously active cause accompanying and aggravating the process of breakdown. Mismanagement is found everywhere: in the third world, where it maintains extremely low levels of life; in the Soviet Union, where it represents, perhaps, an entail from the Tsarist administration, and made Andrei Amalrik ask himself whether the Soviet Union will last until 1984; and in the developed nations of the West, where it protects inefficiency and infects their growing congestion like a deadly germ. Anyone proposing and actively fostering large plans for the healing and improving of modern society ought not to minimize the virulence of this plague, this rottenness (to use the violent expression with which Luigi Einaudi branded the institution of the Prefecture); nor may he disassociate himself from reforming projects and purges such as any good manager would include in his program, when undertaking to restore a failing industrial concern to health.

XIV

The Beginning and Duration of the Dark Age

Variations in different countries

"Did you know that the number of crimes committed in a city each year is proportional to the number of churches there?" Put this to a number of people and you find that most of them immediately deny its truth; some will be greatly astonished. Only a few realize at once that whether it is the city's annual number of crimes or the number of churches that it contains, both are proportional to the population of the city in question, and they will not accuse you of gratuitous impiety or irreligion.

There are many other examples, of course. The number of deaths from street accidents each year is approximately proportional to the number of passengers traveling or miles traveled by the cars of the area. The number of factory accidents is proportional to the industrial production of the nation in which the accidents happen; but the proportional constant is much lower in places where security regulations are more stringent or more rigorously applied.

There are nevertheless some notable exceptions to this last principle. From 1946 to 1967 the number of really big fires that took place throughout the world was forty-five. Exactly one third of these happened in the United States, whereas there were none in Italy, Russia, or Poland. A simple and plausible explanation of this fact can be given, of course; in the United States houses built of wood are more common than elsewhere, and it follows that once a fire gets started in a city, it easily assumes huge proportions. I think, however, that this simple explanation is too simple, and that there is another which is weightier and more convincing. Everyone knows that the recognized ways of fitting electric appliances in the United States are more cautious and exacting than in eastern and southern Europe; above all, there are rules that are scrupulously and effectively observed in America, whereas in Italy, Russia, and Poland they are "more honored in the breach than in the observance." For example, in eastern and southern Europe it is not uncommon for a chandelier to be suspended by the very electric wires that carry the current to its lamps, or for a two-wire cord to be fixed to the wall with screws going through the plastic insulation. In America such improvisations are practically unknown. American consumers regard their electric fixtures as completely trustworthy, therefore; and as a result they expect electricity of superfluously high power to be available to meet all their requirements. This means that the levels of protective intervention (in the fuses) are inordinately high, so that when there is an accidental short circuit the safeguards are not adequate and there is every chance of a fire. Electricians in countries that are technically less advanced, on the other hand, allow for the fact that the level of public confidence in electrical appliances is low. They therefore arrange that the protective fuses shall function as soon as the power that is strictly necessary is exceeded even slightly. When a short circuit occurs, instead of starting a fire, the current is automatically cut off.

This may seem a trite illustration of the point, and yet it is not. We meet analogous situations in other fields. A Polish or an Italian manager who decides to computerize an administrative system does not really believe in his heart that the new system will work. He therefore preserves—in parallel, so to speak—the former antiquated system which worked by hand, with the result that as soon as the new electronic system is in trouble, he falls back easily on the old one thereby ensuring unbroken continuance of service. The American manager, who tends to have greater confidence—it is sometimes limitless—in the new and indubitably advanced systems that he intends to use, is often left without reserves and may find himself in a very grave emergency, without any system at all.

Mistrust of technology is an attitude that ought to be taken seriously. It has positive value in avoiding grave disasters. This sensible attitude has been abandoned in the Soviet Union, apparently; it was decided that the processing of all economic and administrative data coming from all Russian cities, and even from many of the Soviet republics, would be centralized in Moscow. If the large computer in Moscow should happen to go wrong, officials there will no longer know just what is happening to the economy in remote localities; and officials in Kiev, Irkutsk, and Leningrad will be similarly embarrassed. It remains true, however, that excessive belief in technology is a phenomenon most typically American.

The megalopolitan concentrations of people on the Atlantic and Pacific coasts of the United States and in the region of the Great Lakes around Chicago owe their high density and their very existence to the highly advanced technology available to them. The preceding paragraphs suggest that this state of things involves high risks: indeed, it seems probable that the initial manifestations of the coming dark age will be in the United States.

One by one European countries will experience similar regressions to medievalism. To the countries of the American continent (other than the United States) this will happen later—not only because concentrations of people are greater in European countries than in Canada and Latin America, but also because the migration of Europe's scholars across the Atlantic (the brain drain) will have its damaging effect. This phenomenon was already disclosing itself toward the end of the sixties, because of the economic recession in the United States and of the resulting cuts in the grants intended for advanced research there, either from private corporations or from government organizations and, in particular, NASA. Technologists, scientists, engineers, research workers, and managers of European origin who had formerly emigrated to the United States would try to exploit their capabilities anew on returning home to their respective European countries, devoting themselves to activities like those they had pursued in America. Even in difficult economic conditions they would find big corporations ready to welcome them, if for no other reason than that their productive technological know-how—revolutionizing existing systems and creating new ones—might be just the cure for unemployment and difficult economic conditions. All this would contribute to the growth of systemistic concentrations and to the increasing probability that the great systems would reach the state of instability in Europe that had already been responsible for the new medievalism in the United States.

The first phase of the coming dark age, then, would begin in the United States. The second phase would follow a few years later—perhaps five—in the countries of Europe, and in this order: Germany, Holland, Belgium, France, Austria, Italy, Britain, Spain, the Soviet Union, Portugal, Czechoslovakia, Hungary, Poland, Romania, Yugoslavia, Greece, Turkey.

Britain is seventh in this list of European nations because her development was virtually static from 1960 to 1970, when the British GNP grew so slowly—only 20 per cent in the decade. This, however, is not the ugly portent it may seem to be, since it actually defers the British arrival at instability. A significant contrast comes from Germany, where the GNP for the same decade was increased by about 70 per cent after being about equal to Britain's in 1960.

The list does not include Sweden because—as we noted with reference to her postal system—in that country science, technology, and industry are very advanced, while the people are not much concentrated in cities, the population density being eighteen inhabitants to the square kilometer (i.e., about 10 per cent less than in the United States and 11 times less than in Italy). Sweden, with eight million inhabitants (i.e., fewer than London), leads the way in the generation and transmission of electrical power, with very high tension lines carrying direct current. Sweden, therefore, will not be subject to grave crises in its systems and will be an island of efficiency and (perhaps) of continuing progress in a world of regress and death. The climate will help her to remain uninvaded by peoples in flight from the ruin of their own civilizations. The continuing success of this Scandinavian nation, coinciding with the paralysis and breakdown of greater nations, will bring Sweden back to the rank that she had in the tenth century when her influence reached the Black Sea, and in the seventeenth century when she was the greatest Protestant power on the European continent. In the year 2000 Swedish officials will be governing New York, Moscow, Berlin, and Paris.

In the other hemisphere the dark age will begin in Japan, perhaps even earlier than in the United States. During the last quinquennium her production, exports, and urban concentration increased at an annual rate of 10 per cent, whereas devaluation proceeded at the annual rate of 17 per cent. This nation is hastening toward instability.

Another interesting question is the duration of the imminent dark age. I have already defined "dark age" as the period elapsing between the time in which maximum overshoot is reached and the time when the low point is passed and a new period of expansion will begin. It is clear, however, that these large-scale phenomena of regression with expansion to follow do not permit a forecast of much more than the probable *kind* of thing that will happen.

One could argue that the migrations of peoples that may

take place will be more rapid than they were sixteen centuries ago, that historical, scientific, and technical data will remain accessible to quite a large number of people, and that, in consequence, every collapse of prevailing cultural levels will be easily, or at least rapidly, reversible. Such considerations suggest that the imminent dark age should last about a century. It should last slightly longer in the United States, where the new dark era will begin earlier than elsewhere. The subsequent renaissance could start almost everywhere—in Brazil, Mexico, Argentina, China, Japan, and Sweden—but it seems more probable that there will be a convergence of similar phenomena in places far distant from one another, since it is very likely that one of the fruits of our present civilization that will not be lost will be rapid communication, at least by radio, even if not by satellite. (The point here is that during the dark age there will be no organization able to ensure the periodic replacement of stationary satellites.) And if ideas can be communicated quickly, the new civilization will be able to arise with uniform aspects in countries differing and distant from one another, since our only imaginable renaissance must necessarily imply the existence of a movement of new ideas.

Toward the end of 1972 there were certain random indications that the economic recession that had been the experience of almost the whole world might be drawing to an end. But then the worsening of the international monetary situation suggested that the recession would be continuing for some time. If this conjecture turns out to be right, economic and technological development will slow down, the large systems will stop growing (or will grow more slowly), and the final crisis may be delayed for a while. After the recession a new boom will come, and this one or its successor could lead to instability and collapse.

The dark age will have already begun, some time between 1985 and 1995.

XV

Short-Term Gains and Long-Term Losses

In 1870 Marshal Karl Bernhardt von Moltke won a resounding and decisive victory over the French Army. For the French this was not simply a military defeat but a much more profound sequence of upset and collapse. To this general collapse the name *débâcle* was given, and it was used seventy years later to describe very similar events.

The Italian military defeat of 1943—accompanied, too, by the immediate annihilation of all forms of public organization and independent social life—has been popularly described for many years by an onomatopoeic expression, *patatrac* (crash).

The Anglo-Saxon peoples' experience includes no such calamitous events in rapid succession. In English terminology, therefore, the crash of empire has traditionally been described as "decline and fall," whether the theme was the Roman Empire (Gibbon) or the Third Reich (Shirer).

On the hypothesis already suggested that the imminent dark age may begin in the United States, accompanied by the deaths of tens of millions of people, the term adopted to indicate such a huge and immediate breakdown in that country will probably be current coin in other countries where analogous disasters may take place shortly after. It is very unlikely that the classic term *hecatomb* will gain currency, since very few Anglo-Saxons are familiar with it. It seems more feasible that an expression used in another context might be employed, such as the boxing term *knockout* (abbreviated KO). It recalls *blackout,* the word used for the great failure of electric current in November 1965, and it was used a quarter of a century ago for darkening lights during the war. The wartime blackouts, however, were carried out by government order: visible lights—whether public, private, or fixed to vehicles—were forbidden. The blackout of 1965, on the other hand, involved the complete absence of electric power; and, similarly, the future KO will be an event much more tragic than the fate of a youth who falls to the ground stunned because he has received a blow on the jaw. In the remaining chapters of this book I shall use the abbreviation KO, and in this chapter I shall list the material advantages that should occur immediately after the KO, and the losses in ever greater number that will affect those who survive at a considerable distance of time thereafter.

It is clear that there is no point in speaking of advantages and disadvantages in some future situation, as though opinions on the subject could be unanimous. Look, for example, at the Anglo-French project for the production of the supersonic aircraft Concorde. Professor Mishan would probably consider its eventual abandonment intrinsically and socially advantageous, mainly because no supersonic planes would mean no sonic booms, and life would be more peaceful. On the other hand, the directors of Rolls-Royce, the company that would be making Concorde's engines, would consider that a decision to ban the project was a definite confirmation of the failure of their company, harmful to progress and to the long-term well-being of the English people and of the whole human race. If, however, the directors of Rolls-Royce should be convinced that they would not be able to sell more than twenty Concordes (instead of the two hundred necessary for them to show a profit), they could then agree with Professor Mishan that without Concorde life would be more peaceful. However, this peace would be due not to a low noise level but to their acceptance of the fact that the revival of Rolls-Royce, its restoration to health, were now impossible.

When I speak of the advantages of the KO, therefore, I am not implying that they will be equally available and desirable to everyone surviving the KO, but only that an appreciable percentage of survivors will benefit.

There is one fact that will bring notable relief to many survivors: the grim problems facing them will at least be completely different from those that have been tormenting them in past years. The problems of an advanced civilization will be replaced by those proper to a primitive civilization, and it is probable that the majority of survivors may be made up of people particularly adapted to passing quickly from a sophisticated to a primitive type of existence. Such survivors will not have too much regret for what has been destroyed (since at first the main victims of destruction will be structural forms, functions, and organizations rather than buildings and places), nor will they grieve excessively over their friends and relatives who died during the KO. It is normal experience that single calamities are felt to be much more tragic than catastrophes that hit very great numbers of people. And this is not only true of those catastrophes that occur in far distant places. It is not only the 500,000 dead in Pakistan or the 200,000 dead in Biafra who leave us somewhat cold: even the death of a relative in the crash of an airliner is felt to be less tragic than the death of the same relative in a light aircraft.

The first benefit to be enjoyed by the survivors will be the end of congestion: there will be too few people left in circulation to cause any congestion at all. One must point out, however, that many who now deplore the oppression, injustice, and intrinsic ugliness of life in a technically advanced and congested society will decide that things were better when they were worse; and they will discover that to do without the functions proper to the great systems—without telephone, electric light, car, letters, telegrams—is all very well for a week or so, but that it is not amusing as a way of life.

To some of the survivors it will be an obvious advantage that so many durable goods will be available in excess of demand. The death of the greater part of a city's population (once the corpses have been removed) will make houses and dwellings of all types available far in excess of need. If, before the KO, there had been on an average one car to every two inhabitants of a city, after the KO there will be some two or three cars per head, and for a time the survivors will be able to satisfy their transportation needs simply by using one of the many abandoned vehicles. The car industry will disappear. Later, when old cars have been used up and there are no new ones, abandoned cars will be the obvious source of spare parts, until new needs begin to renew industrial production. Then, production will be on a small artisan scale, fulfilling small commissions or making single parts.

Buildings will show a similar gradual breakdown—an initial superabundance resulting in the disappearance of building as a great industry. A small number of people, forced to rely on themselves, will be unequal to the adequate maintenance of the buildings they are using; and they will give no attention at all to those they are not using. Empty buildings will be raided for fixtures or odd pieces having some structural value; and this, along with damage due to weather, will cause collapses. These will bring down other, inhabited buildings. In the long run, therefore, houses will be much scarcer than they were before the KO, and new ruins will become a typical feature of the urban landscape. Ancient and noble ruins will be covered and obliterated by new ones in accordance with a process that was familiar in the former Dark Ages. Vandalism will add to collapse and destruction in cities; and inasmuch as it will not cause direct harm it will not be punished, but will be one of the few entertainments still available to the young.

After the KO, as during the original Dark Ages, the distinction between new and secondhand objects will lose the great importance that it has at present. The only distinction will be between things that are effectively usable and those that are broken and beyond repair. Again, this will happen at first because of the availability of many secondhand things in good condition. Then new objects will become extremely rare, so that there will no longer be anything derogatory about the term "used." Further, new products will often be of much poorer quality than used products made of better material and in accordance with finer methods of production. Before the KO the standard of living reached by a large number of people in the advanced nations made it respectable for them to buy books and antiques secondhand, but certainly not clothes: to acquire a used garment was almost unthinkable. After the KO used clothes would not only be bought or bartered; they would be heirlooms. One hopes that at least this new state of things will gratify today's detractors of consumerism and all who are annoyed (perhaps not unreasonably) that fashion should be so powerful in the field of consumer goods so that people will buy a new car only to possess the latest and most elegant model, not because the old one was performing badly.

A very severe restriction of the movement and use of cars will follow from the scarce and irregular availability of oil products and gasoline. As a consequence, journeys for pleasure will become very rare and will be reserved for the powerful or for tramps who will have to go long distances on foot. There will be a large increase in the percentage of people who have never moved from the place where they were born, neither for work, nor for sightseeing, nor for any other reason. The scarcity of travelers will provide opportunity for the revival of brigandage. Pilgrimage will be the motive for undertaking fairly long journeys. Indeed, we may expect that the new dark age will favor the revival of a religiosity as simple as it will be widespread, and expressed in forms that today are unforeseeable. This, incidentally, could be listed among the advantages of the KO by anyone who believes that religion—however, wherever, and at whatever level it finds expression—is a good thing. Anyone, on the other hand, who regards religion as false and harmful will put every revival of the religious spirit, along with magic and superstition, into the list of disadvantages—already long enough. For any surviving ethnologist a new efflorescence of primitive culture in his own city would be manna. For historians and sociologists also, a regress of modern civilization on the grand scale would be a unique and fascinating phenomenon which, despite the inconveniences and risks involved, could be classed as *vaut le voyage* (worth it).

In the next chapter I shall widen the discussion somewhat: first, by looking at new and degenerative social forms arising *before* the KO, and representing not only an apprehensive awareness of its initial manifestations but also an attempt to prevent it: second, by looking at new forms of social life *after* the KO.

To return to our present theme of the KO and its effects: In the field of economic relationships an important element in the modern consumer structure that will be missing at once is credit. In conditions of extreme instability, no one could possibly give a creditor meaningful guarantees of future payment with interest. It is very likely that at first all forms of money will lose whatever value they have and that exchanges will be solely by barter. Their intrinsic rarity will suffice to keep gold and silver coins in use, and the old convention would be re-established whereby the weight of coins and ingots would be the sole determinant of their value: every merchant would include in his office equipment a small balance for weighing gold and silver. It would be very interesting, above all for specialists, to try to foresee how banking structures will develop after the KO, what monetary policies (if any) there will be, and what economic cycles will be like. Such attempted forecasts, however, could not be anything but a gratuitous exercise, if we reflect on how difficult if not impossible it is today to make much more short-dated forecasts, and without having to take into account exceptional events such as the KO. Furthermore, the whole economic situation and structure will be heavily influenced by new legal and judicial structures about which also there is little to say save at the level of imaginative anticipation.

Other short-term advantages can accrue to the so-called developing countries inasmuch as they are actually subject to, colonized by, or oppressed by more advanced countries on their way to regression. When the regression of the advanced nations becomes effectively obvious, their oppression of others will cease and the less developed nations will experience relief. But it will probably be brief, because in the long run much graver problems will emerge, not only because finished products from the regressing countries will then be lacking, but also because generalized armed conflict is likely to be the pattern, either between nations in retrogression, or between those that have not yet advanced, or—at a more microscopic level—between cities, villages, or families, and between individuals.

XVI

Social Life Before and After the Knockout

When the Organization for Economic Cooperation and Development (OECD) recommends to all or to some of its member governments energetic and concrete measures to improve things in the field of economics, technology, and education, its suggestions are rarely given a prompt welcome. In some cases, when it is feared that the suggested measures may be particularly unpopular, the OECD is virtually forced to dilute its wine with a good deal of water and to expurgate its documents, censoring dangerous or offensive sentences, or reducing its principal statements to harmless generalities. There was an occasion of this kind in the late autumn of 1970 when the OECD suggested to the governments of Europe—in very cautious circumlocutions—that the one remedy for the sad economic conditions in their respective countries was an increase in unemployment. The specific rightness of OECD's remedy remains to be demonstrated, and it is possible—as Lord Beveridge would have asserted magisterially—that it cannot be; but the one fact that I wish to emphasize is that

the OECD report was not published until the passages
about unemployment were very tactfully censored, without even being discussed.

UNESCO supports too many soothing initiatives that
are often expressed in language so vague as to recall the
prose of *Reader's Digest*.

The United Nations withdraws its troops when a situation becomes desperate—this happened immediately before the Six Day War—and allows the armed conflict that
is just beginning or has already begun to proceed without
hindrance.

People need mutual help and co-operation. These international organizations, each designated by its sequence
of capital letters, seem unable to meet this need. Public
bodies—governments, local authorities, and corporations
—rarely achieve the purposes that they were set up to fulfill. I ought not to deny, of course, that there are many
organizations and systems that still function reasonably
well; but our list of grave problems is always growing
longer, and solutions to them are every day receding rather
than approaching.

The financial and economic difficulties of most Western
countries—balance of payments, inflation, unemployment,
productivity—are worsening, and the machineries devised
to control them can do nothing to stop the rot. America
is not solving its grave problems of individual and group
violence nor its impending problems of pollution and of
disposal of city refuse. In almost every European country
deficiencies at the municipal level are much more evident
than in America: there are too few doctors, hospitals,
schools, streets; there is not enough use of electronic ap-

paratus and not enough servicing. These tendencies are becoming more marked, and they seem to indicate that before very long it will be to the obvious and indisputable economic advantage of private groups to undertake public works at their own expense. The money that private individuals pay in rates and taxes is ill spent, and fails to provide the works and services presupposed by such payments. This is what happens in Europe, which is still without the American system of voting bonds. These are communal allocations of funds based on future communal imposts that will be authorized by public vote. It is almost inevitable, therefore, that new communal organizations will arise in Europe, too, taking the place of inactive public authorities and providing the services that no one else will.

Vigilantes are groups of armed citizens who ensure public order in certain cities of the United States. Their specialty is the night patrol, an emergency service for outbreaks of disturbance or sedition. Sometimes they have extremist right-wing tendencies. A political and moral estimate of vigilantes is not our concern here. We should notice rather that the people belonging to these groups will not be disposed to continue paying taxes and rates for the employment of police who are inefficient (or are presumed to be). They may dispense with such services, replacing them with their own action.

Along the same lines a group of citizens in Europe restores at their own expense the worn surfaces of the streets where they live. They have their own small-truck organization for throwing garbage, etc., into the nearby river; they assume responsibility for a public job, finding their reward in a usefulness that only the group can offer but that it willingly makes available to the large majority of people who are not members. This group will sooner or later refuse to pay taxes that (in theory only) buy these same services. Refusal to pay taxes is the first step toward becoming politically independent of a central government and of antiquated local authorities—not to mention those international organizations that seem to have no perceptible authority. At first the budget program of these new community groups will be limited to certain exclusive activities; then they will develop a stable constitution and, for a certain time, they will be highly efficient, thanks to their originating motive—a realistic determination to reach certain concrete short-term ends.

One may assume that in coming years new communes (or whatever these new private forces of co-operation may be called) will begin to emerge in several countries, their characteristics being everywhere much the same. The resemblance to one another of these forms of human association will be mainly due to the convergence of like with like, rather than to a contagious spread of ideas. That is, the new co-operatives will arise spontaneously, called into existence by the standard failure of public authorities to be alive, effective, and up-to-date.

In various ways these new communities might successfully revive efficiency, bringing plan and method into administration. They might apply psychological pressure or even use violence to make the existing setup function better. They could organize a time-sharing movement on a large scale, using resources that are in short supply by rationing them between different users at different times.

Let us turn briefly to some of the issues raised by the rapid growth of population, taking figures from the United States as our starting point. According to data supplied by the U.S. Census Bureau, the population is now over 200 million and immigration is at the rate of 400,000 annually. In A.D. 2000 the population could be a maximum of 320 million (every woman producing, on average, 3.1 children), and a minimum of 240 million (with immigration abolished and every woman producing, on average, 2.11 children; i.e., the number of births just enough to equal the number of deaths). Let us suppose that the actual figure will prove to be somewhere between these two limits and that the population of the United States will grow to 300 million by the end of the century. On this hypothesis—with the way of life there remaining much the same—all civil structures (houses, transport, systems for producing power, communications, administration, medical care, systems of distribution, schools, etc.) will themselves have to increase by 50 per cent. This means constructing the equivalent of an entirely new city of 280,000 inhabitants every thirty days during the next thirty years. A good part of the problem would be solved if time-sharing were adopted, working hours being staggered throughout the day, days off throughout the week, and vacations and holidays throughout the year. In the same rational way planning could drastically reduce congestion in transport, communications, and the utilization of energy by some 20 or 30 per cent. Other systems of time-sharing have been suggested. Though even less attractive and more unpopular than those already mentioned, they too might offer striking advantages: the same dwelling houses could be used at different times by different people, one shift working by day and the other by night.

We need not continue the list to convince ourselves that such rational and collectivist measures are so inherently distasteful that governments for a long time to come will not be in a position to compel their adoption. Even the efforts made by communities themselves along these lines will have only marginal successes. (The one form of time-sharing that seems to be popular is adultery, but it is hardly suitable for solving these problems.)

The possible rise of new communities, then, can only delay the arrival of grave conditions of instability and the crisis of the knockout. It will not change the general tendency very much. If the new communities come into existence before that crisis, they will have enough vitality to continue to exist in the dark age; and it is conceivable that they will be able to conserve knowledge, traditions, and motivations onto which, after some lapse of time, the subsequent renaissance would be grafted.

It is certain that free societies would have no easy time in a future dark age. The rapid return to universal penury will be accompanied by violence and cruelties of a kind now forgotten. The force of law will be scant or nil, either because of the collapse or disappearance of the machinery of state, or because of difficulties of communication and transport. It will be possible only to delegate authority to local powers who will maintain it by force alone—and who will be able, with the same force, to resist the source from which their delegated authority derives. In such a situation feudal anarchy becomes the rule.

The rights of property will undergo very profound and

rapid changes. Registers of landed property—even now chronically inaccurate and out of date—will lose all meaning: at first because most landowners will have died without heirs, and then because perpetuating a grievous and antiquated system of property registration is an intolerable burden when that property is virtually worthless. Ownership through use will become the common way of acquiring property; it will no longer require ten or twenty years or more to be operative, but a few months or weeks. The advantage of possession will make most desirable these properties which easily lend themselves to defense against seizure by force. Buildings or lands girt with walls of some thickness will be particularly suitable, since the firearms used will be conventional and probably light. Dwellings will come to look like castles or redoubts, strongholds with armed courts giving shelter to dependents, clients, and associates. The siege may return as an important tactic.

Though modern firearms will be available, physical strength will also be important. It will be necessary in man-to-man combat, in trifling day-to-day emergencies once dealt with by machines, and also in handling obstacles caused by nature or the enemy.

One imagines that military units would remain in existence indefinitely, since the KO would find them functioning with proper discipline and already having the use of defensible and well-supplied positions. But the probability that this normal situation would last is very slight. In fact, if a unit happened to be in an inhabited and civilized area, the KO would induce its members to disappear home. On the other hand, if the unit found itself in a remote and inaccessible area from which it could make no easy getaway, it would remain compact, unbroken, and even disciplined; but once isolated, it would have no effective power and no contact with the majority of survivors. Whether or not it continued to exist would not be very important.

The new architectural forms that will be imposed upon earlier structures will be less important than new ways of meeting the needs of housing, defense, and trade, in armed tenements or in the few free communities that will be incapsulated within the iron reality of an age of violence. As in the sixteenth century, the acute-angled bastion may become typical—a good defense against artillery fire and well adapted for placing its own firearms in favorable positions. There will be no special significance about the uniforms and other features worn by people who will assume military command; familiarity with arms is always notoriously favorable to the distinguishing evidence of badges, caps, tunics, belts, facings, and plumes.

Feudal structures will emerge, of the type where one's authority is delegated from above but depends directly on one's own powers for its effect. The balance of authority between distant center and local potentate will therefore be based on intricate and fleeting compromises. These structures, new only in appearance, will openly recognize a state of things already in existence before the KO, and masked only by empty forms. Illustrations of this are found today not only in Oriental countries where tribal powers are hidden in parliaments identical with Britain's; even in the better democracies the real power is not always held by the one who can impose it with arms. After the KO many such fictions will no longer be necessary.

It would be easy to suggest a comparison, or perhaps an identification, between such feudal and oligarchical structures as I have mentioned and the huge organizations like the Cosa Nostra, the Mafia, the Calabrian Fibbia, and the Camorra. These secret organizations attract attention today (i.e., before the KO) because of the violence they use in a relatively nonviolent epoch, and because of the undue power they exercise in accordance with private rules. These rules are unwritten and not publicized, and they appear to have hidden and disgraceful links with men who represent the power of the law and are, perhaps, in the government. My point is that after the KO it will be all one Mafia. Governments will rarely draw their power from free elections—fraudulent or not—and almost every center of power will have its origins in compromises and personal contacts.

Personal relationships, friendships, and useful contacts will become more important than they were before the KO. It is common experience that during times of famine, disaster, chaos, and war many men behave like wolves to their fellows, inflicting on them any harm from which they can gain some advantage. But at the very same time many other people get into the habit of offering help and services freely, even to complete strangers. Something like this happens today in Eastern countries where public services either do not exist or are quite unreliable. No one trusts the postal system, and letters and parcels are therefore carried by hand, by acquaintances and travelers. The inns are few, and travelers find hospitality, therefore, in the houses of acquaintances, or of perfect strangers. Similarly, during the blitz, Londoners lent their houses to those without a roof; and in Sardinia, until a few years ago at least, anyone finding himself in an area where there were no restaurants or eating places had no option but to have himself invited to a meal—without payment, of course—with some family of notables. The sense of solidarity and the habit of showing hospitality to the unknown passer-by were widespread and indisputable a thousand years ago; they have been handed down to us in many popular songs with a pilgrim as hero, and are diffused throughout hippie communities today because they live by choice in permanently adverse conditions.

It is to be anticipated that material hardships, the unexpected grimness of living conditions, and the sheer contrariness of things will occupy some people's time so intensely that the prevailing cultural levels will necessarily be low—a nadir from which the best exemplars of civilization in the period preceding the KO would have prayed to be spared.

One desire above all wells up spontaneously within us, therefore. We yearn to discover whether there are any possibilities of preventing the dark age from happening. Admittedly our directive and organizing resources are inadequate. The tendencies and developments of our time seem unlikely to achieve the effective change that would enable us to work our way gradually to conditions of stability and to escape crisis and catastrophe. Despite this doubt, however, our longing to avoid the regress to a new age of iron compels us to investigate what would be the measures and initiatives necessary to win a more acceptable goal. We must make the investigation, even though we may find that there is no one who can take these measures and these initiatives.

XVII

Foundations of a New Tradition

This is not a chapter in a book about the shape of things to come. It is a manifesto, a call, a sermon—delivering its somber discourse in the manner of Luigi Einaudi, who regarded his last writings as useless even before the public had delivered the same verdict. Naturally enough, exhortation is not expected to go against the grain and to urge a new tradition of efficiency in opposition to the established tradition, so old and cozy—which encourages the majority of people to take the line of least resistance, to make do with compromises, to substitute improvisation for long-term and exacting reforms, and to let the blunders of top people go uncriticized and their authority unchallenged.

In Italy this tradition is felt to be typical of our country, but it is no less present and alive in other countries; just as the members of each profession feel that the density of incompetence is at its maximum in their own group only because information about its defects is more fully available to them.

The difficulty of creating new traditions recalls the story

of the American who asked an Oxford don what would be required to establish a university such as Oxford in the United States; the answer was "Money, a very able body of teachers, a good constitution, and about eight hundred years."

But even with a few centuries at our disposal it is doubtful whether we should succeed in reversing current attitudes or practices and in halting what—paraphrasing J. K. Galbraith—we may call conventional ignorance. And yet this is one of the few hopes we have of making an effective stand against the breakdown of the great systems. There are certain specifics that would allow us to achieve this aim, and it is worth stating them exlicitly and in order:

1. Cases of flagrant incompetence should be denounced by those who know of them. Judgment should be by arbitration, and be much sterner than the situation may strictly require, since reforms (or counter-reforms) succeed only if their reach exceeds their grasp, only if they are ruthless, and only if they put the fear of God into the culprits.

2. The mild and tolerant way in which scientists and other professionals assess, review, and back one another's work should be outlawed. We should dismiss the objection that brisk criticism—uncongenial in academic and professional circles, especially the notorious exclusive professional societies—would only lead to sterile controversy. Better that some controversy be sterile than that there be none at all. Dog should eat dog. The situation to which this change could give rise could certainly be nasty, but without it there is no salvation.

3. However odious the word "religion" may be, a high

and inflexible standard of moral judgment should be restored as a *religion* in schools and universities and in appointments to high office. High standards should be cherished for their own sake and not because of their desirable social consequences; otherwise a justification will always be found in the end for whatever is average, and a lowering of the standard in cases presumed to be special. The recognition that errors of judgment have been made through excessive optimism should therefore be considered a merit, and it should lead equally to a reversal of judgment and to a lowered status for those who have been overvalued.

4. What I am aiming at is, clearly, a higher and more exacting standard of professional conscience, or a stiffening of the superego, to use the terms of dynamic psychology. As H. J. Eysenck has argued very plausibly, the conscience that defines what is evil and prevents us from doing it does not derive from a learning process but from a conditioning process. It seems necessary, therefore, to begin to condition people to more stringent standards of conscience from a very early age; that is, in our primary and secondary schools. To me it seems indisputable that such measures are necessary. If education in the first years of life is not prearranged but imparted haphazardly, its results will themselves be random and, mostly, bad.

More generally, we must increase the number and the worth of our institutions of education, our schools and universities, because not only the level of civilization but also the economic and industrial success of nations and, in the long run, their very survival are bound up with the quality and the amount of education they succeed in producing. It is in the first as well as the second of these criteria that the United States is way ahead. There are over twelve hundred universities in the United States—that is, one university to every 170,000 inhabitants—granting degrees after courses lasting at least four years. The most important fact here, however, is that the number of those who attend these universities is a very high percentage of the population: 43 per cent of those aged between twenty and twenty-four. The corresponding percentage of the same age group is only 24 per cent in the Soviet Union, 15 per cent in Britain, 13.5 per cent in Japan, 16 per cent in France, 7.5 per cent in Germany, and 6.9 per cent in Italy.

It is true that in recent years there has been severe criticism of American universities, even by the students and professors who belong to them. It is also true that, in Europe, critics of American universities commonly console themselves by urging that the standard of some of them is very low. But here we must not forget that we can apply to American universities the laws of large numbers, whereas this cannot be done in the case of other countries. Even if it is true that there are several American universities of low standard, there are others almost equal to them in number that are of outstanding excellence, and a multitude on the average level in between.

The importance of these universities cannot be expressed only in figures or in statistical comparisons. The fact that they are the best in the world can be shown simply by making a list of twenty of the most famous: Harvard, Yale, M.I.T., California Institute of Technology, Carnegie Institute of Technology, Illinois, Columbia,

Michigan, California at Berkeley, California at Los Angeles, Stanford, Cornell, Princeton, Chicago, Texas at Austin, Duke, Ohio State, Northwestern, New York University, and Johns Hopkins.

Nevertheless, the numerous symptoms that we have already mentioned and discussed indicate that it is in the United States that the imminent dark age will actually begin. We are therefore forced to conclude that the world's most advanced, ambitious, and intensely utilized educational system will not suffice to avert this fateful breakdown and to establish a needed new tradition in its stead. Education could bring great betterment, raising on a vast scale the contribution that the populations of advanced countries could make to the world and reversing the present tendency toward breakdown in the large systems. But this could only be the outcome of an educative force almost unimaginably powerful. It is a force that should be inordinately successful, making even the most ambitious of present-day plans seem of little account. But there is no indication at all that anything like this is happening; and so the situation looks irreversibly desperate.

International organizations and committees of so-called experts fail even to see what the real problem is: namely, how the advanced countries should use their resources. Such organizations concentrate their energies on the unreal problem of educational backwardness and defective know-how in underdeveloped or developing countries. It is true, of course, that the backward majority of the world's population cannot keep pace with the advanced minority, and that in the fields of education and management as well as of technology this gap is bound to grow wider. But these are secondary aspects of the real problem, which is continually getting worse. Its dramatic issues are the reverse of what is commonly supposed: the gap is closing, and the most advanced nations today are going to be steadily less able to fulfill former functions of guidance. Only in decreasing measure will they be able to provide economic aid, finished products, and know-how.

Serious and relatively modest projects for reforms and educational innovations that ought to be realizable are already running into great and insuperable difficulties. And yet (as we have already noticed) any project that really could establish a new tradition in opposition to contemporary regression would have to be "maximal" by definition: but this, its essential characteristic, would prevent its being accepted and put into practice.

The dilemma is insoluble. But a blunt recognition of this fact is no answer to the simple question: What is to be done? For however much the situation may have worsened, we cannot simply abandon any attempt to anticipate the future and to bring more rational influences to bear upon it. Indeed, our attempts might meet greater success the more our starting point is realistically pessimistic.

As for better-placed managers or technocrats who have greater resources at their disposal and have faced problems similar to those we are analyzing, we should wait in vain to hear any voice from among them—sufficiently pessimistic, subtle, and authoritative—that would make proposals worth attending to, or able to sustain plausible hopes. Managers and technocrats are spoiled, perhaps, by their successes in certain limited areas: they are accustomed to the optimism and oversimplification that are inapplicable to realities.

For instance, co-operation on a world scale, which Aurelio Peccei specifies as essential, would require not only the agreement of governments but also their effective initiative. And anyone who has had a taste of the bureaucratic delays of public bodies and has reflected on the failures of government planning (Russian five-year plans, aid for depressed areas in Italy, plans for new cities and integration projects in the United States, production targets in Cuba) has good reason to doubt whether any enterprise involving not just one government but many is practicable. Peccei rightly underlines the systemistic character of the most critical problems that society has to face; and he writes that "humanity and its environment constitute an integrated macrocosm, i.e., a world system." But we have seen that many a partial and more modest system has developed in such a way as to be less rather than more subject to control—a fact that should make us aware that humanity may lack not only the economic means and the will, but also the tools, brains, and schemes needed to run a world system.

Alvin W. Weinberg, director of the nuclear laboratories at Oak Ridge in the United States, has described population growing more rapidly than the means of subsistence as "the first Malthusian dilemma." He adds that "the second Malthusian dilemma" is the proliferating complexity that accompanies the growth of population in technically advanced countries. Malthus had assumed that the means of subsistence grow only in arithmetical progression while population, if uncontrolled, grows by geometrical progression. Weinberg, speaking approximately, says that the number of semantic contacts (by communication, transport, transmission of power, conflict) grows as the square of the number of people concerned. For the first as for the second Malthusian dilemma he sees simple and cheap technical remedies, for which he has coined the expression "technological *fix*." (A fix is an aid, an antidote, an arrangement, a quick solution—pragmatic and prefabricated.)

Weinberg's doctrine, set out in his book *Reflections on Big Science* (1967), proposes schemes much vaster than simple textbook solutions, and they can look convincing to technicians or to people generally who tend to trust in purely technical solutions.

He asserts, for instance, that overpopulation can be mastered by the diffusion on a wide scale of Gräffenberg's interuterine contraceptive coil; but a rudimentary version of this very simple "fix" has been used by courtesans since the fifteenth century, and there have been no appreciable results so far.

Again, according to Weinberg, the availability of nuclear power at very low cost would make the desalination of sea water possible and, as a result, the irrigation of huge uncultivated areas that could provide food superabundantly to meet every necessity.

The technological fix for war is already discovered. Weinberg means the H-bomb; the ultimate deterrent, dissuading governments from embarking on military adventures. Yet it did not serve to prevent the war in Vietnam in which the United States lost more aircraft than in World War II.

Finally, Weinberg maintains that the information explosion could be harnessed with the fix of an appropriate use of large computers. They would eliminate the summertime unrest of blacks in American cities, calming tempers by means of lower temperatures obtained through massive air conditioning. This last idea in particular is ridiculously naïve; but it is more serious that Weinberg has not even tried to propose technological fixes for city congestion and instability. The availability at an extremely low price of power produced at great nuclear centers does not solve the problem of the stability of electrical networks. The congestion of traffic in the streets could be sensibly alleviated by forbidding the construction of cars more than six or seven feet long; but no one wastes time in estimating the advantages obtainable from a measure so unpopular and controversial.

Attempts to solve social problems do not appear to be on the way to better success, thanks to the application of managerial techniques and of systems analysis "proper to the space age." In 1965 the Democratic governor of California invested some hundreds of thousands of dollars in study contracts assigned to industrial companies that had scored great successes in the space field. Lockheed projected a system costing $100 million for the collection and centralized investigation of all classifiable data in the state of California (economic, organizational, bureaucratic, technical, legal, and environmental). The North American Rockwell Corporation studied the state's transport systems and suggested that certain mathematical models of simulation should be developed. The Aerojet General Corporation was busy over the disposal of refuse and the prevention of crime, and succeeded in defining a three-year program for planning the necessary systems at executive level. All these studies brought no concrete action of any kind and were ignored by the Republican successor of the Democratic governor who had commissioned them.

In 1969, after fruitless years, came the failure of the plan conceived by Litton Industries at the request of the Greek colonels' government: it was supposed to attract foreign investment of some $400 million and to aid the economic development of the more depressed areas in Greece.

The proposals and efforts of Peccei, Weinberg, and the space-age industrialists ought not to be disparaged. We must hope that they will have successors to rival and surpass them, since there is no alternative—unless it should be seriously decided to plan monastic communities for conserving the essential elements of our present civilization during the imminent dark age. Our concluding chapter is devoted to this theme.

XVIII

Monastic Communities Looking
Backward and Forward

Julius Caesar, Cicero, Diodorus Siculus, Pappus of Alexandria, and Martianus Capella did not spend time drawing up plans for founding the universities of Oxford and Cambridge, of Bologna and Rome—institutions founded many centuries after they were dead. These universities have had a notable influence on man's cultural development from the twelfth to the twentieth century, albeit with varying fortunes. This is incontrovertible fact. And yet it would be absurd to blame the statesmen, scholars, and cultivated men of antiquity for not having foreseen and prepared for university foundations.

To use eschatological language, Julius Caesar, Cicero, and the others saved their souls because they could not foresee "the imminent dark age" and could not even imagine the conditions in which the founding of universities would be spontaneous and significant.

If in our day we foresee that a new medieval epoch is approaching, we shall not be able to save our souls without anticipating as best we can what measures could be taken and what structures set up to save things in our civilization that we value most, and to facilitate the new efflorescence of a culture that, though certainly different from this one, may preserve at least certain of its characteristic traits—possibly the best.

We ought to be more intensely aware of this responsibility the more we realize that we cannot escape from a process that seems to lead almost inescapably from the congested conditions in which the most advanced masses of men now live to conditions of instability, and thence to a crash, a knockout. On the other hand, there is always some element of uncertainty in our predictions; and those that I have just been making are no exception. We ought not to neglect the hypothesis, therefore, that the most advanced countries may, in fact, *not* go all the way toward the developing instability and may not have to endure some grave crisis that will widen out into a new medieval- ism. This optimistic hypothesis is not a very likely one, for it would require the sheer reversal of too many of those tendencies that everywhere dominate the way in which the world runs its commerce, industry, schooling, cities, nations, and all other human groups.

That things may go well after all, then, seems an un- likely hypothesis. But if, despite this improbability, the conditions that we have called dark or medieval do not materialize, would not organizations devised and ready to function during the darkness look silly after a time? They would look no sillier than many an armed force does in time of prolonged peace (and sometimes, unfortunately, in time of war too). It may be that soldiers are trained not to worry if they do look silly; or is it that they are clearly distinguishable from people with no sense of humor? The point is that it would be appropriate in any case to have organized groups charged to conserve certain data and certain civilized forms, and to foster a new beginning when the right time for it comes, in such a way that they would be fulfilling useful functions even if there were no apocalyptic crisis after all.

It could be argued that organizations meeting these very requirements already exist, fulfilling this valuable cultural role, standing ready for any disaster, and conserving what is best in contemporary civilization: universities, centers of learning, modern research institutes, all do this. And anyone maintaining this could find soothing justifications. If (they would say) our directives, our way of life, and the forms of culture we actually enjoy are the best possible—and they clearly are or we should have changed them by now—it is proper that people should go on doing what they are doing now; and the result will be good, whether the general situation continues to be largely normal, or whether disturbances of a medieval type break out.

That this point of view is fallacious should be clear to all those who have been warning us of the crisis in colleges and schools, and to anyone who reflects that the very inadequacies of college and school are a remote cause of the future crisis that we may expect from now on.

These groups that I am contemplating—conservers of civilization and catalysts of a future renaissance—should have characteristics in common with monastic fraternities, if only because they would have to differ profoundly in constitution and purpose from the way of life, the distress, and the disorder prevailing in society outside. This differentiation would naturally be best guaranteed by monastic isolation. But it is not worth drawing an exact parallel between these new groups and the monastic communities of the Dark Ages long past. There is a widespread notion that the classics, Greco-Roman civilization, and the uncorrupted Latin tongue were conserved in medieval monasteries; and in a sense this is certainly true. Yet the fact remains that many interesting classical texts were lost there, scraped and rubbed away from their parchments with pumice stone so that psalters and sacred hymns of very minor interest might take their place; and it is certainly arguable that Thomas Aquinas rendered no good service to Aristotle. But this is not the essential point. I shall be borrowing from medieval monasticism no more than its name, and I shall not be contending that the name presupposes the thing behind it.

The new monks would have to conserve knowledge, and the memory of the ways in which certain things are done, if we assume (rightly, as I think) that the very concept of culture implies both knowing and doing (*savoir faire*). One of the main purposes in conserving such data could be to transmit facts about certain events and situations to future historians. The "time capsules" that have been devised in the United States are a present-day example of this attempt to conserve the present for a far distant future. They are airtight and watertight: indeed, they are so made that they are impervious to heat and to all such external agencies of change. They contain printed texts, pictures, samples of artifacts and manufactures, and are intended to be rediscovered some thousands of years hence. The making of such time capsules is redundant and superfluous, however, since the conservation of data destined for future historians is already securely prearranged in the encyclopedias and similar voluminous records produced in all advanced countries and printed in very large numbers. Printings of such works exceed tens of thousands of copies—sometimes hundreds of thousands —and this single fact ensures that some of them at least will remain intact. To be preoccupied with selecting the best books, etc., and preserving them in the safest and most protected places, would be a mistake. All that would be worth doing in this respect would be to produce special ad hoc reports containing information that is so common today that it would occur to nobody to record it formally in a standard encyclopedia; whereas the same data might be lost and impossible to reconstruct in a future context of life that might be totally different. It is not easy, though, to imagine just what data are in fact neglected in this way, whether in encyclopedias or in contemporary books.

But the conservation of knowledge could have another and more interesting purpose—that of maintaining available ideas, theories, and procedures so that they might be utilized to reconstruct forms of civilization and social life that have been destroyed or have perished. In other words, this would be a way of initiating the renaissance. And here I must say explicitly what I mean by the term.

I define "renaissance" as a situation of reborn well-being, or of productivity again increasing to such levels as to permit many people to devote their time wholly or largely to study, learning, or research—no longer condemned to unending utilitarian drudgery in order to make sure of sustenance, shelter, and survival. Renaissance can mean, simply, a big increase in the percentage of educated people of a certain type; and there would be no point in seeking to define their characteristics precisely. Any anticipation of what the imminent dark age will be like is necessarily blurred and vague; a remark that applies with even more reason to what may be expected to come after it. One cannot even show formally that the renaissance will be preferable to what will precede it or that it will be alto-gether desirable. Renaissance is an end to be pursued by any who deem it desirable, and this is almost all that may be said about it. Or, indeed, about any ends that men may set themselves. One cannot really refute, for example, the banal argument that we ought not to worry over making the future better for posterity since posterity will certainly do nothing for us.

In the imminent dark age people will endure hardship, and for the greater part of their time they will be laboring to satisfy primitive needs. A few—perhaps one in ten thousand—will have positions of privilege, and their work will not consist in battling personally against adversaries, or in cultivating the soil, or in building shelters with their own hands. It will consist in schemes and intrigues, grim-mer and more violent than anything we know today, in order to maintain their personal privileges and to increase their personal power over others. Almost no one will be free from immediate burdens and able to think with de-tachment about abstract and general issues.

The groups conserving civilized values and preparing for the renaissance will have to enjoy notable freedom from the immediate anxieties which would otherwise exhaust their energies; and this could happen only by means of an initial endowment made soon enough (that is, before the dark age actually begins) by the planners of the survival groups. This initial endowment could not be in money, since money will obviously be among the first of the various casualties when the systems break down. Instead, it would have to be an endowment of concrete things: tools, implements, motor-generator sets; nonperishable goods which a monastic community would make more of; goods exchangeable for food, particularly salt, sugar, and alcohol; drills, electric cells, copper wire, stainless steel screws, and small-arms ammunition.

Groups for survival will be found competing ruthlessly with other survivors of every sort gathered in chance clusters. To be clearly and effectively privileged they will have to be in possession of a huge initial endowment, possibly of such a kind that only certain governments could control it. Government intervention could at least solve the problem of finance, but its slowness and inefficiency would give rise to numerous other problems. It would be open to pressures from interests that the Establishment of the day had constituted earlier, and from the inevitable—and at present desirable publicity to which it would be exposed. A significant example of such embarrassing difficulties was provided some years ago when governing circles in Britain attempted to plan a network of anti-atomic shelters and a complete organization for guaranteeing the survival of the machinery of state, and the safety, security, and support of certain key people in case some enemy should make a nuclear attack on the British Isles. The plan was that the following people should be quickly conveyed to safety: the royal family, the government, several high functionaries and technocrats, certain high-ranking members of the armed forces, and a corps of secretaries, technicians, and executives, including a *corps de garde*. It appears, too, that in order to ensure the efficiency of many of these people during the state of emergency, the plan also provided for conveying their families to safety, so that heads of families might devote themselves to their work without additional strain and anxiety. But the preparatory work for these emergency procedures had to be interrupted—or perhaps continued in greater secrecy —because the Campaign for Nuclear Disarmament found out about the scheme and began a public discussion of its morality. The obvious question was: By what criteria were those who were to survive selected?

I do not know whether the criteria used were particularly open to criticism. There is no doubt, however, that criteria free from objection would be impossible to find. The composition and structure of these groups for survival would have to be decided by a specialist. Apart from the fact that specialists in this field do not exist, it is clear that every individual's interest in survival, and in being included in one of the groups, would be so strong that every decision as to particular individuals would be automatically suspect.

The problem of selecting the type of culture to be conserved, the ways in which to do it, and the people to be entrusted with realizing them is certainly not soluble on a democratic basis. One solution, therefore, could be trust in free competition—the hope that free competition would result in the conservation of types of knowledge, and in the survival of conserving groups having diverse and even opposite characteristics.

The monastic communities for survival will be located in high places, because in a dangerous age it is heights that are easiest to defend. They enable the advance of hostile forces to be seen from a distance and prepared for; and they favor the traditional counterattacks that are helped by the force of gravity—the rolling down of rocks and stones against assailants. Further, hilltops are naturally protected against floods; they are also very likely to be left alone by large masses of people on the move, since migrant hordes are inclined to go after easy prey rather than undertake an arduous siege of doubtful outcome.

Having an initial endowment, and being predisposed to resist rapid changes in the world around them, will be an advantage so great that communities for survival could exploit it for ends different from those that they were instituted to achieve. In fact, heads of such communities will be exposed to a continuous temptation to become actively involved in conflict and to reach a position of primacy, possibly in a remote geographical area isolated from the rest of the world. Such a development ought certainly to be avoided, since it would be very unlike what such communities were initially constituted to be—that is, to conserve, and then to act as catalyst or liberating factor in a vast movement of rebirth.

Still, no designer of systems could determine beforehand all the possible mutations and variants that communities for survival would experience in a life that, it is hoped, would be long. Consequently it will be proper to rely on statistics—or, better, the laws governing large numbers—and to begin with the founding of as large a number of communities for survival as possible, accepting the hazard that some may disintegrate and disappear; that others may forget the purpose for which they were founded and become transformed into baronies or centers of brigandage; and that, in the end, only a few may respond effectively to expectations—conserving the structures and learning worth conserving and acting constructively for the rebirth that is to come.

The communities of this last class could be compelled to live in secret for quite long periods without disclosing any indication of their true nature. This could happen, for example, in particularly dramatic fashion if the community were surrounded by the flow of migrating populations or of invaders from distant lands. The science being preserved would then run the risk of becoming crystallized, losing all vitality, and being gradually transformed into empty formulas of steadily shrinking significance. Much later on, people more vigorous and more gifted than their predecessors could arise, who would want to rediscover the true meanings and real functions of the learning in their books, and of ways of doing things transmitted to them by routine practice and by word of mouth. The risk at this point will be that the reconstruction may be a travesty of the original learning, serving only to give birth to an untrue and artificial copy of the civilization surviving from our day. Revivals of this kind, whether faithful or not, seem destined to have a short life: the Emperor Julian's reconstruction of the Roman religion, for example; or the second French empire. There would be little interest, therefore, in a painstaking effort to say just how people in the future might imagine, or make a working model of, an older world altogether different from their own.

The real problem for the men of the future will be to extract knowledge useful for their several concerns from a heap of data not immediately relevant. The quest for information accumulated in the past presents difficulties almost as serious as research into what is being produced and printed continuously in publications too numerous to be gone through. After the knockout many truths and many inventions will be discovered for the second time, because finding the records of previous inventions at the right moment would be impossible. This phenomenon, by the way, is with us today too, *before* the knockout, on a scale so vast as to be hardly imaginable. Too many young scientists and technicians are restricting their own documentary references, to books and reviews published during the last ten years, because they regard earlier work as out of date. To begin the task of evaluating old and outdated textbooks would be a useful apprenticeship that certain survival groups might select as one of the short-term aims to be pursued before the knockout.

The new monasteries would not be able to function in the way projected if they limited themselves to conserving fixed formulas, or to ensuring that texts were complete and unmutilated. A priesthood that regarded the books, microfilm, or magnetic tapes in its keeping as so much sacred furniture would be fulfilling functions useful only to future archaeologists. Difficult though it is to define it formally, effective continuity in learning will be assured only in an unbroken succession of able individuals whose habit of mind, power of intellect, sense of tradition, and constructive interest are constantly being reproduced.

The vitality and efficiency of the survival groups can be entrusted simply to their statutes; that is, to a set of rules drawn up initially to define the tasks and scope of the order, the method of choosing new candidates for recruitment, procedures for delegating and transmitting authority, the structure of the group, the duties and rights of its members.

Alternatively, one might include in the structure of the groups a sequence of automatic controls, entrusting the monasteries not with the explicit function of conserving knowledge and know-how, but with long-term and ulterior ends impossible of attainment unless the scientific know-how is already available and usable. The strictest and most paternalistic way of realizing a structure of this type would be to split up into separate lots the endowment assigned to each group. These would be hidden from and inaccessible to any candidate for membership who proved unable to use certain technical tools and to keep them in working order, or unable to interpret and solve certain cryptic ciphers presupposing the use of mathematical, physical, and chemical theory. Candidates' quests for these lots into which the whole endowment would be divided would not be a simultaneous operation: it would be staggered over a period of time. This could be done by automatically timing the release of the successive clues in code for locating and identifying each cache. Admittedly, this way of providing would-be members of survival groups with a motive—prizes in kind, the scheme being a sort of treasure hunt—might smack too much of artifice, and would depend on timing mechanisms that could hardly be absolutely reliable. Moreover, the mechanisms would have to be known to be mined, so as to dissuade treasure hunters from trying to jump the line and get premature hold of lots intended for the future. To maximize an immediate yield in this improper way would be to sabotage the scheme as a whole and destroy its program; the orderly transmission of future benefits cannot be ensured unless the period during which your potential technology may become actual is carefully phased and extended.

It would seem preferable, then, to assume more disinterested motives in the survival groups, leaving them free to decide just how to make use of the huge free gift with which they would be initially endowed. Faced with new and unforeseeable facts as they may arise, each group should be free to choose—to say no or yes to whatever new tendency or whatever new force may appear on the scene.

My conjectures about the shape of things to come can be considered simply as an effort to know and to demonstrate what we may expect in coming decades. I have also tried to indicate what action could be undertaken to avoid the knockout, or to facilitate a new renaissance after a dark age. Clearly then, my intention is not only investigation but realization.

Every attempt at realization owes more to the individuality of the people participating in it than to the pieces of paper that specify its purpose and aims. Moreover, new (and irreverent) criteria will be needed for choosing the people to be entrusted with planning measures against the threatening dark age; or, should it be decided that all such measures would be ineffective, with planning underground monasteries, clandestine groups, and *maquis*, pledged to go on existing and to work for the rebirth that will come. Those, for example, who will be excluded will be the repositories of "absolute" truths, false innovators, politicians who are "progressive" and inefficient, vague and misleading prophets, cyberneticians. Included will be certain directors of scientific research, industrial managers, exceptional economists and psychologists, people of sound scientific and social judgment in the professions, farmers and breeders, miners and chemists.

Looking ahead to the imminent dark age can have profound implications for the future of every one of us. It is natural to ask ourselves how our activities, our attitudes, and our personal plans should take account of all this and be modified by it. When ought we to begin getting busy building a family bunker rather than planning our next vacation? To this question and to others like it the preceding pages do not claim to give a better answer than a book on the stock market can offer to a man wanting to play the market.

Nor can anyone tell an aspiring speculator to what extent money really is desirable—for him. And yet there are people who expatiate on ends, trying to prove that there are ultimate goals that every man should desire to reach. There are also many who become disillusioned, losing the faith they once had in certain general good ends —either while still seeing them a long way ahead and pursuing them, or after they have at long last reached them. For these there is no salvation.

Only the man who has successfully served his apprenticeship as a mentally sound person will be able to define just what desirable ends are; and he will be able to attain them only if he is master of the means that they presuppose, and can adapt his actions to the unpredictable changes of real life. Although it would be foolish to ignore the preponderance of chance in deciding the fate of men and the destiny of nations—whether they will survive and even attain to pre-eminence—the only feasible road to be taken is that of preparedness. We prepare as we observe how the physical world and human society function; as we distinguish, and then improve on, what each is capable of doing.

Human societies are going downhill: powerful pressures make his existence increasingly unstable. There would be no sense in trying to reverse these tendencies simply by admonishing society and governments. It is the appeal to the individual that alone can have direct, albeit limited, results. The capacity to learn is undoubtedly present in each individual, and is sufficient proof that—in certain cases at least—making more information available can bring salvation.

Notes

1. *Science, Prophecy, and Prediction*. Harper, 1961.
2. International Publications Service, 1971.
3. *The Prince,* Chap. XXV.
4. *Electronic Design*, Vol. 16, No. 26 (1968).
5. Wright-Allen Press, 1971.
6. *IEEE Spectrum*, August 1968.
7. *IEEE Spectrum*, September 1969.
8. *A Chasm Ahead*. Macmillan, 1969.